E S T A T E   P U B L

GW01237412

ALFRETON · [

MATLOCK · RIPLEY · WIRKS\

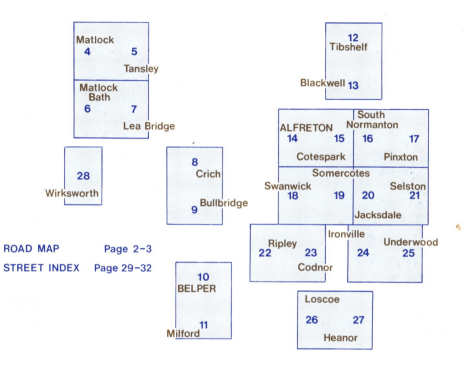

Matlock
4   5

Tansley

Matlock
Bath
6   7

Lea Bridge

28

Wirksworth

8
Crich

9
Bullbridge

12
Tibshelf

Blackwell 13

ALFRETON   South Normanton
14   15   16   17

Cotespark   Pinxton

Somercotes
Swanwick   Selston
18   19   20   21

Jacksdale

Ironville
Ripley   Underwood
22   23   24   25

Codnor

ROAD MAP   Page 2–3

STREET INDEX   Page 29–32

10
BELPER

11
Milford

Loscoe

26   27

Heanor

Every effort has been made to verify the
accuracy of information in this book
but the publishers cannot accept
responsibility for expense or loss caused
by any error or omission. Information
that will be of assistance to the user of
the maps will be welcomed.

The representation of a road, track or
footpath on the maps in this atlas is no
evidence of the existence of a right of way.

One-way Street	→
Car Park	Ⓟ
Place of Worship	✛
Post Office	●
Public Convenience	Ⓒ
Pedestrianized	▨

Scale of street plans 4 inches to 1 mile
Unless otherwise stated

Street plans prepared and published by ESTATE PUBLICATIONS, Bridewell House,
TENTERDEN, KENT, and based upon the ORDNANCE SURVEY maps with the sanction
of the Controller of H. M. Stationery Office.

The Publishers acknowledge the co-operation of Amber Valley D.C.,
Derbyshire Dales D.C., Bolsover D.C., Ashfield D.C., and Broxtowe D.C.

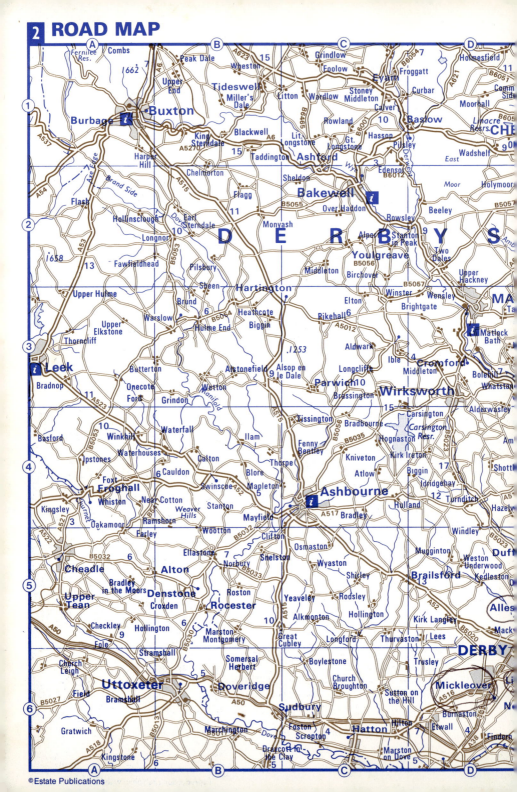

2 ROAD MAP

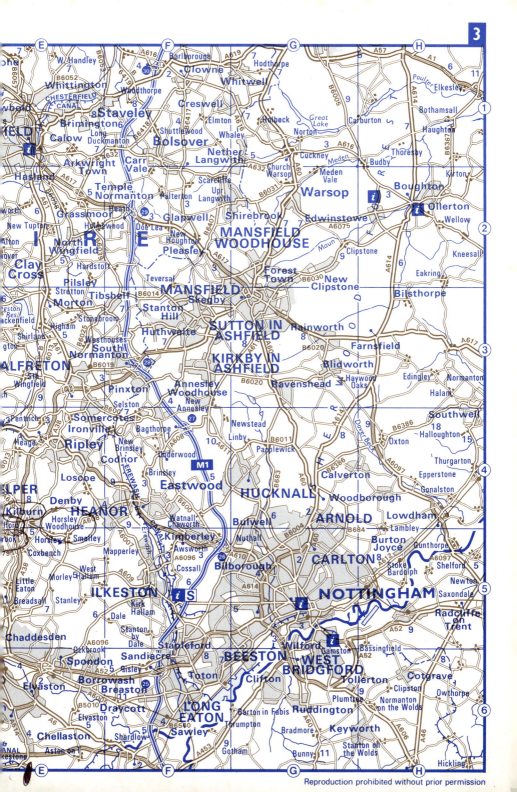

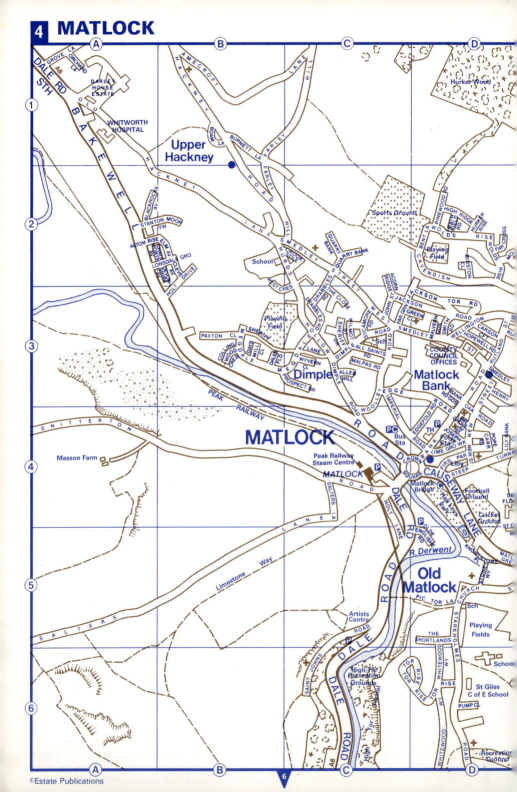

Upper Hackney

Dimple

Matlock Bank

MATLOCK

Old Matlock

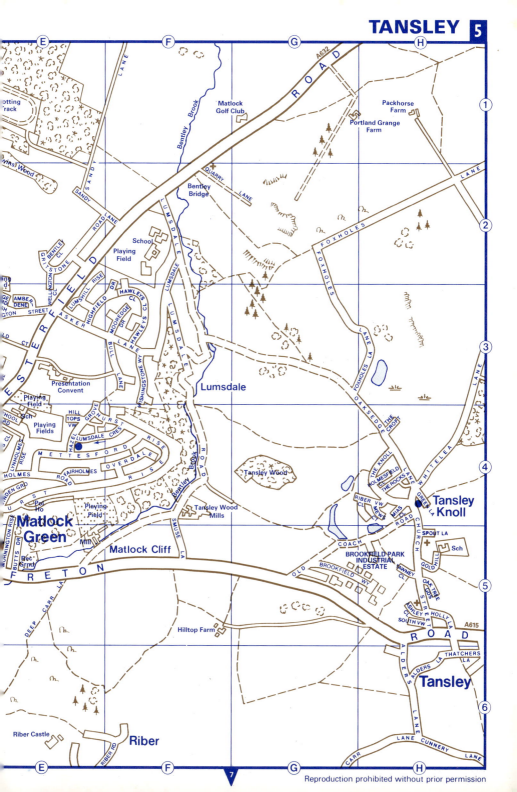

E F G H

1

2

3

4

5

6

A632 ROAD

Packhorse Farm

Portland Grange Farm

Matlock Golf Club

Bentley Brook

Quarry Lane

Bentley Bridge

FOXHOLES

School

Playing Field

BENTLEY CL

GRITSTONE

WELLINGTON

AMBER DENE

LINGTON STREET

FLASKER LANE

LUMSHILL RISE

HIGHFIELD DR

MOOREDGE DR

HAWLEYS CL

HAWLEYS CL

BULL LANE

LUMSDALE

LUMSDALE

SANDY

ROAD LANE

LANE

FOXHOLES LANE

FOXHOLES LANE

OAKSEDGE LANE

WHITELEA LANE

Presentation Convent

WISHINGSTONE WY

Lumsdale

THE CROFT

THE KNOLL

HOLMESFIELD

THE ROCKS

RIBER VW

MEWS

MIAS

GREEN LA

CHURCH

Tansley Knoll

Playing Field

Sch

Playing Fields

HILL TOPS VW

GROVE

HAZEL

LUMSDALE CRES

METTESFORD

FAIRHOLMES ROAD

OVERDALE

HURST RISE

RISE

Tansley Wood

SPOUT LA

Sch

HOLMES

LINDEN GRO

HURST

Pol Ho

Playing Field

Tansley Wood Mills

RIBER

ROAD

COACH

BROOKFIELD PARK INDUSTRIAL ESTATE

BROOKFIELD WY

TAWNEY CL

OAK TREE RDS

GOLD HILL

Matlock Green

Mill

Rec Grnd

Matlock Cliff

SMUSE LA

OLD BROOKFIELD

ASHLEY STREET

SOUTH VW

HOLLY LA

A615

CHESTERFIELD

BUTTS

WARNINGTON RISE

FRETON

Hilltop Farm

ROAD

ALDERS LANE

ALDERS LA

THATCHERS LA

DEEP CARR LA

Tansley

Riber Castle

RIBER RD

Riber

CARR LANE

CUNNERY LANE

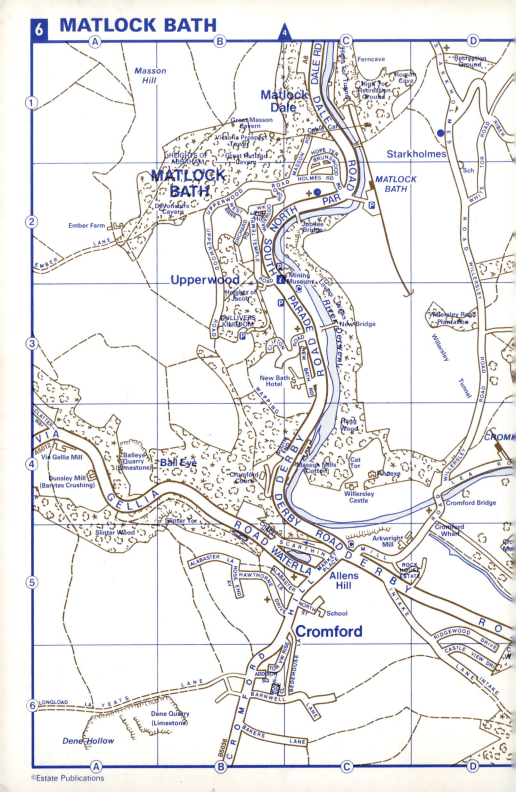

6 MATLOCK BATH

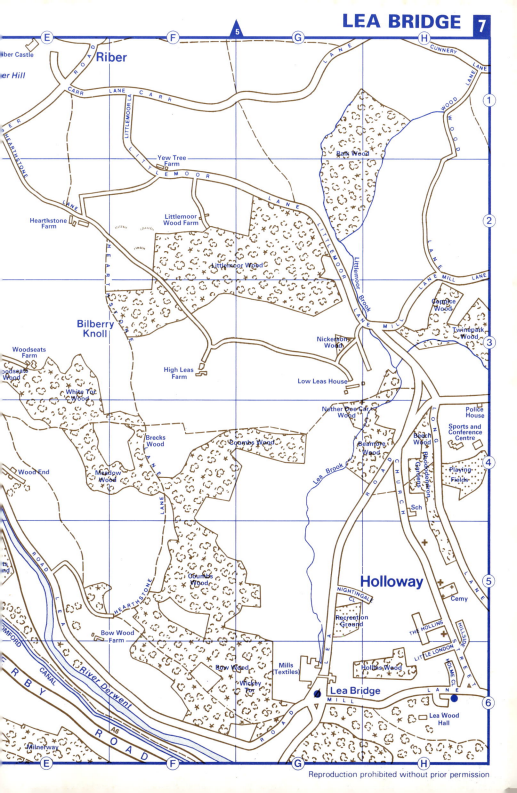

Riber Castle

Riber Hill

Riber

CUNNERY LANE

CARR LANE   CARR

LITTLEMOOR LA

HEARTHSTONE LANE

Yew Tree Farm

LITTLEMOOR

Bark Wood

WOOD LANE

Hearthstone Farm

Littlemoor Wood Farm

LANE

Littlemoor Wood

LITTLEMOOR LANE

Littlemoor Brook

MILL LANE

Coppice Wood

Bilberry Knoll

Nickerson Wood

MILL

Twinepark Wood

Woodseats Farm

Woodseats Wood

High Leas Farm

Low Leas House

White Tor Wood

Nether Dec Car Wood

Police House

Sports and Conference Centre

LANE

Brecks Wood

Coombs Wood

Lea Brook

Beamore Wood

Beech Wood

LONG

ROAD

CHURCH

Rhododendron Gardens

Playing Fields

Wood End

Meadow Wood

LANE

Sch

Coombs Wood

Holloway

NIGHTINGALE CL

Cemy

HEARTHSTONE

THE HOLLINS

HILLSIDE

Bow Wood Farm

Recreation Ground

LITTLE LONDON

HOLME CL

STREET

LEA

ROAD

RAMFORD CANAL

River Derwent

Bow Wood

Mills (Textiles)

Hollins Wood

Wickey Tor

MILL

Lea Bridge

LANE

Milnerway

A6   ROAD

Lea Wood Hall

8 CRICH

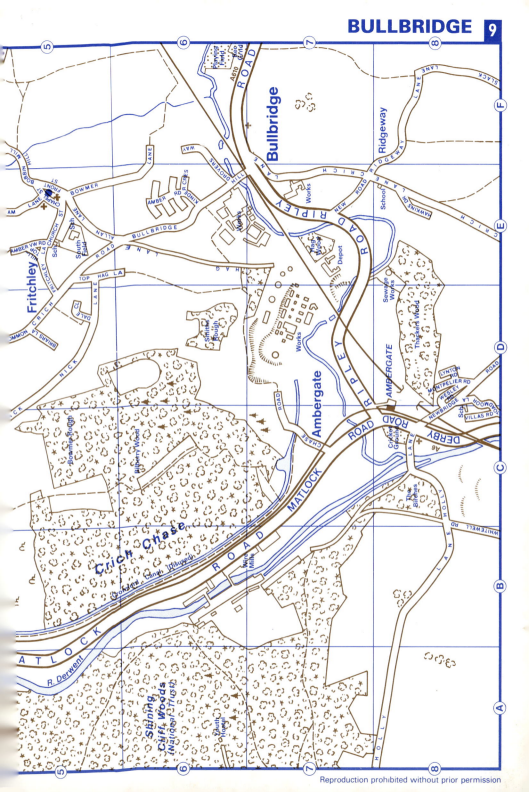

10 BELPER

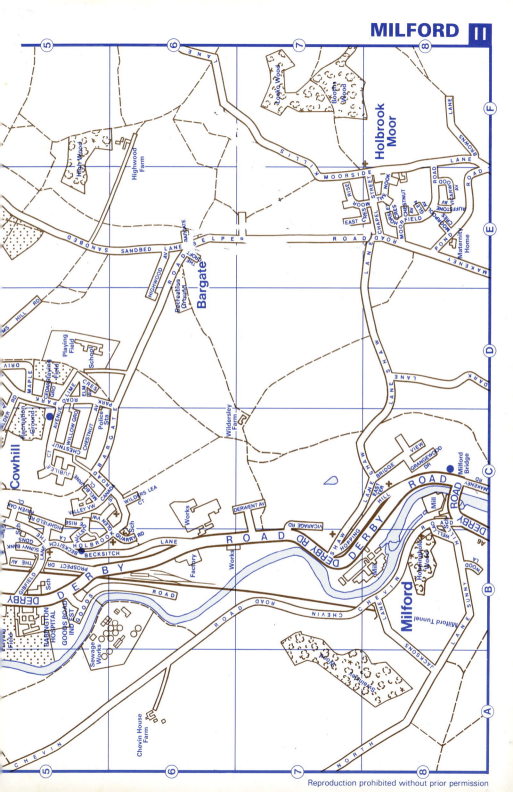

Holbrook Moor

Cowhill

Bargate

Milford

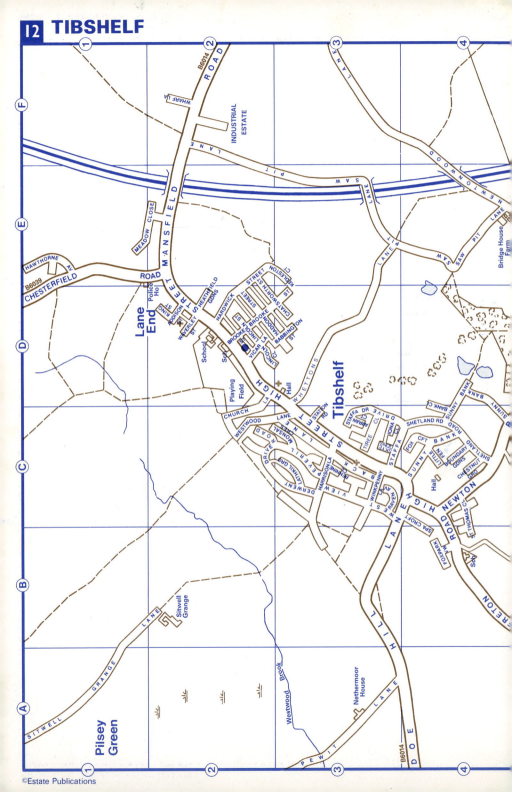

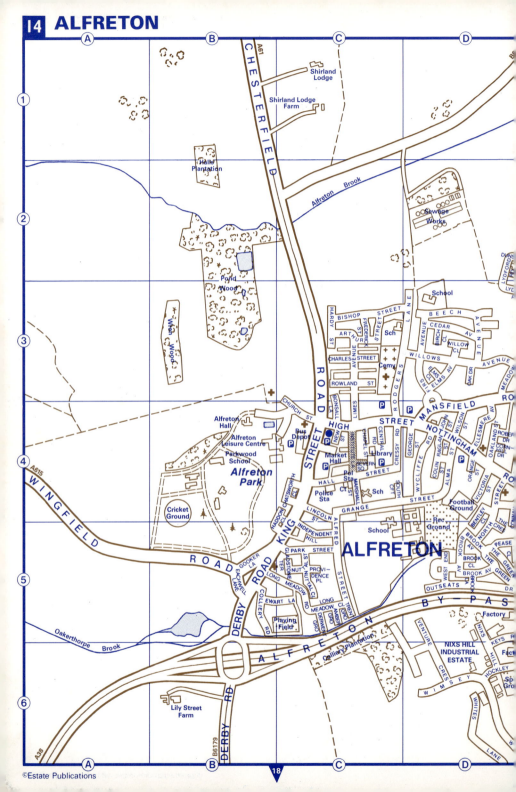

14 ALFRETON

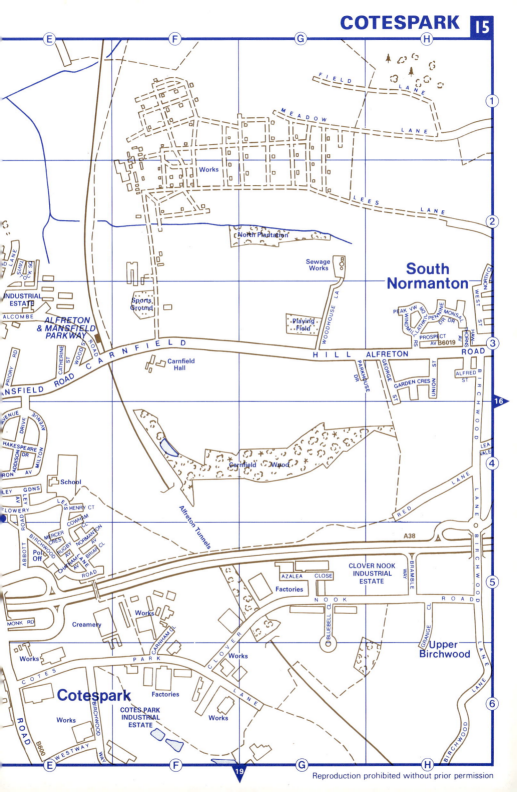

South Normanton

Upper Birchwood

Cotespark

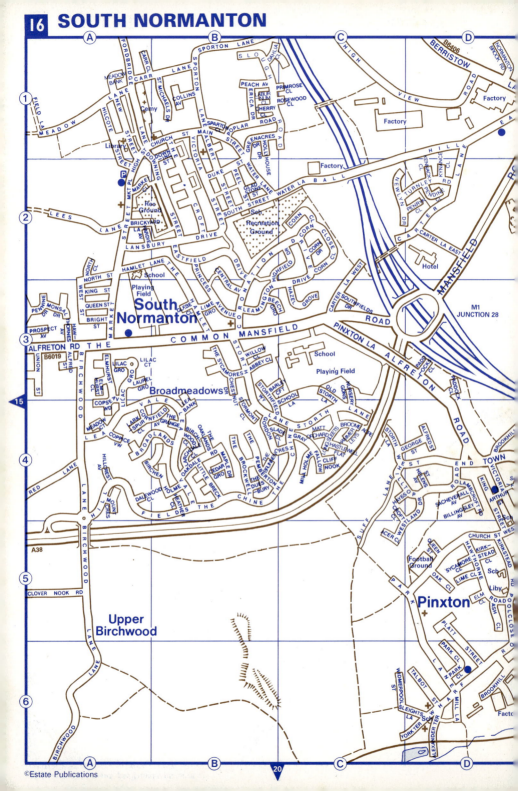

South Normanton

Broadmeadows

Upper Birchwood

Pinxton

M1 JUNCTION 28

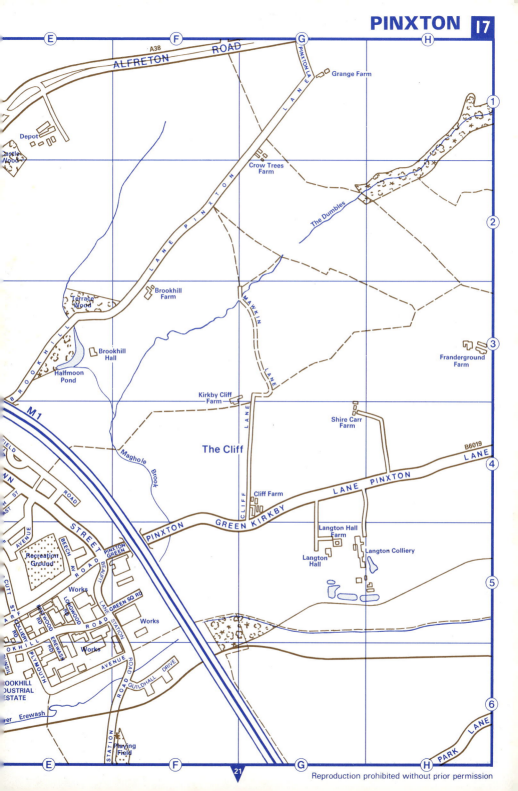

Grid references: E F G H (top and bottom), 1 2 3 4 5 6 (right side)

ALFRETON ROAD
A38
PINXTON LA NE A
Grange Farm
Depot
Castle Wood
Crow Trees Farm
The Dumbles
PINXTON LANE
Terrace Wood
Brookhill Farm
MAWKIN LANE
Franderground Farm
Brookhill Hall
Halfmoon Pond
BROOKHILL
Kirkby Cliff Farm
Shire Carr Farm
The Cliff
M1
Maghole Brook
CLIFF LANE
B6019 LANE
LANE PINXTON
Cliff Farm
Langton Hall Farm
Langton Colliery
PINXTON GREEN KIRKBY
Langton Hall
STREET
ROAD
Recreation Ground
BEECH AV
LONGWOOD ROAD
PINXTON GREEN
BEAUFIT LA
GREEN SO RD
Works
Works
Works
AVENUE
STATION ROAD
GUILDHALL DRIVE
BROOKHILL INDUSTRIAL ESTATE
River Erewash
Station Playing Field
PARK LANE

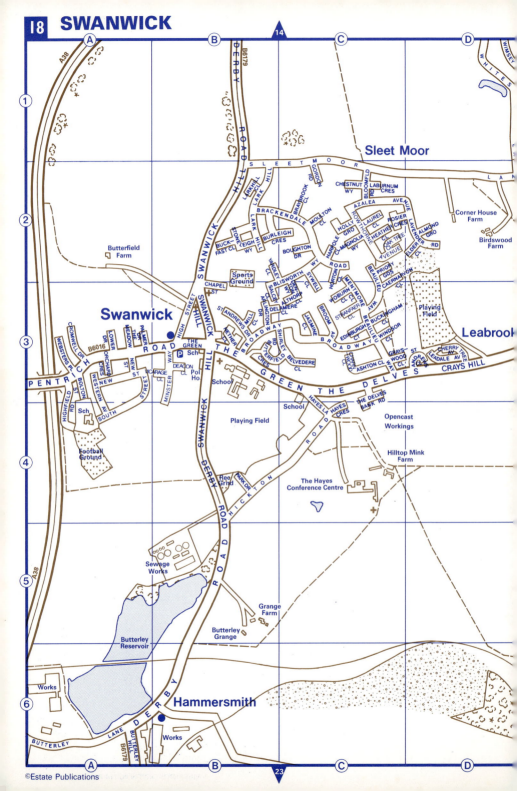

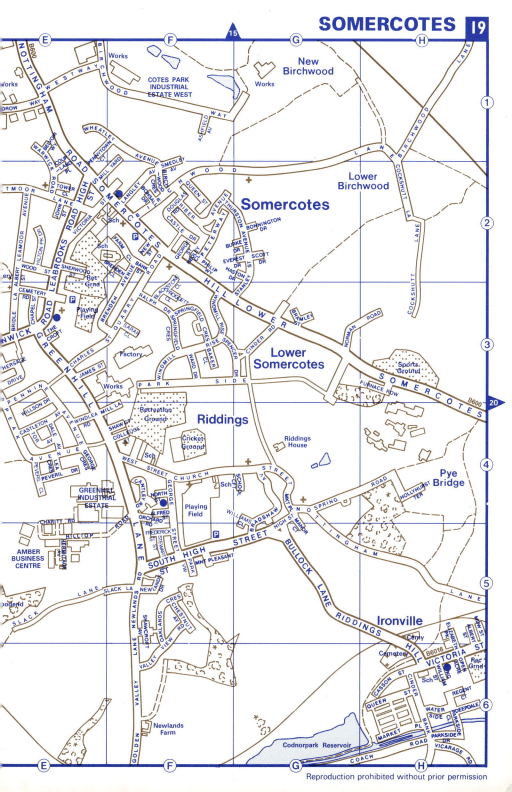

Somercotes

New Birchwood

Lower Birchwood

Lower Somercotes

Riddings

Pye Bridge

Ironville

COTES PARK INDUSTRIAL ESTATE WEST

GREENHILL INDUSTRIAL ESTATE

AMBER BUSINESS CENTRE

Riddings House

Sports Ground

Recreation Ground

Cricket Ground

Playing Field

Codnorpark Reservoir

Newlands Farm

A   B   16   C   D

1

Pinxtonwharf

Sewage
Works

2

River Erewash

Selston
Green

3

LWR
SOMERCOTES
B600
MAIN   ROAD   ALFRETON   ROAD   ALFRETON
19

Playing
Field
Pye
Bridge

CHURCH

ST HELENS DR
SYCAMORE CR SPRL
GREEN
FARM RD

HOME FARM
CT

Gol
Cour

Sewage
Works
4

Pye
Bridge

Toadhole

ROAD   LANGTON   HO

CRESCENT

LANE

BARROWS

Works

5

NOTTINGHAM

Codnor Park
Junction

Colliery

Burrows
Green

WAGSTAFF

LANE   PALMERSTON   ROAD

ALBERT

STREET   PYE

NEW
ACCOMMODATION
RD

Pye Hill

SELSTON

KIT-
SON
AV

Recreation
Ground

NEW   WESTWOOD

VICTORIA
Bridge
Recreation
Ground

KING WILLIAM   STREET

LAVERICK

FRANKLIN

ROAD

ROAD

BARKER   WESTDALE
AV

RUTLAND   WILTSHIRE
AV

DERBYSHIRE
DR

CHESHIRE
WY

Recreation
Ground

School

6

Ironville

HILL

ROAD   MAIN

WAGSTAFF   LANE

ALBERT   AV
EDWARD
YORK

HAMPSHIRE
CT
KENT
AV

SHROPSHIRE
AV

RUTLAND

ROAD   CUMBERLAND

STREET   MAIN

Westwood

Westwood
Gardens

Cromford   Canal

(Disused)

Jacksdale

DIXIE   STREET

THE
ORCHARDS
ST

SEGWICK
WEST
MORLAND
WY

RUTLAND
WY

CORNWALL
AV

A   B   24   C   D

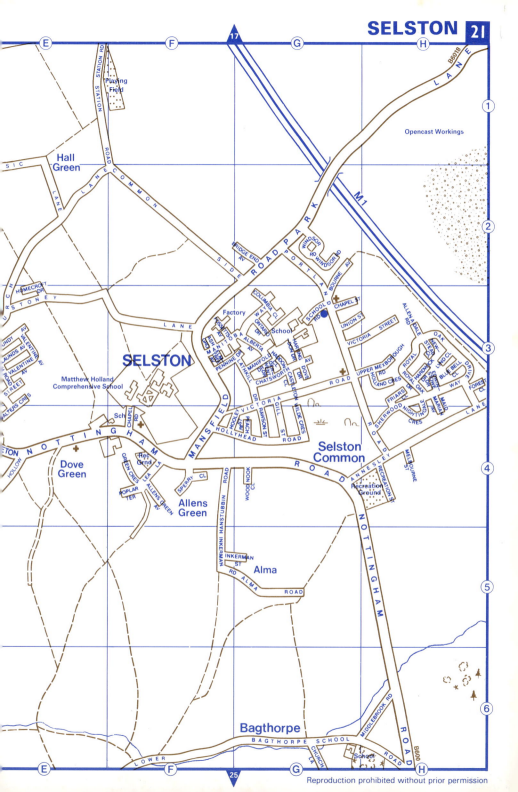

Hall Green

Playing Field

STATION RD
STATION LANE
ROAD COMMON

Opencast Workings

M1

B6018 LANE

HOMECROFT DR
CHURCH
SIC
STONEY

LUNDY AV
VALENTINE AV
LAUNDS AV
VALENTINE AV
STREET
WALTERS CRES

SELSTON

Matthew Holland Comprehensive School

BRIDGE END AV
SIDE
ROAD PARK
PORTLAND
WINDSOR RD
WINDSOR RD
BOURNE AV

LANE

Factory
School
COLUMBIA CL
WAY
ASH
MANITOBA
ALBERTA
ONTARIO
PENNINE DR
MANIFOLD
LATHKILL
CHATSWORTH
DOVE
HARDEN
CASTLETON
WILDE CRES
GILL
CHAPEL ST
SCHOOL CL
UNION ST
VICTORIA STREET
UPPER MEXBOROUGH
HOLLAND CRES
ALLENDALE RD
ASH
OAK
STEAD
MAPLE
ROYAL OAK
ROYAL
HARDWICK ST
LIND CL
BLUE BELL CL
DRIVE
OAK
FOREST CL
WAY

FRIARS CL
SHERWOOD
NIGHTINGALE
MAID MARIAN
NOTTINGHAM
MANSFIELD
HOOLEY
VICTORIA
PEACH
RAWSON ST
ROAD
HOLLYHEAD

Dove Green
CHAPEL RD
Sch
Rec Grnd
GREEN CRES
ALLENS GREEN
LA
POPLAR TER
SPERRY CL
WOOD CL

Allens Green

Selston Common
ROAD
ANNESLEY
MELBOURNE ST
Recreation Ground

HOLLOW
ETON

HANSTUBBIN
INKERMAN
WOODKIN

Alma
INKERMAN ST
RD
ALMA
ROAD

NOTTINGHAM
ROAD
B600

MIDDLEBROOK RD

Bagthorpe
BAGTHORPE SCHOOL
LOWER
CHURCH LA
School

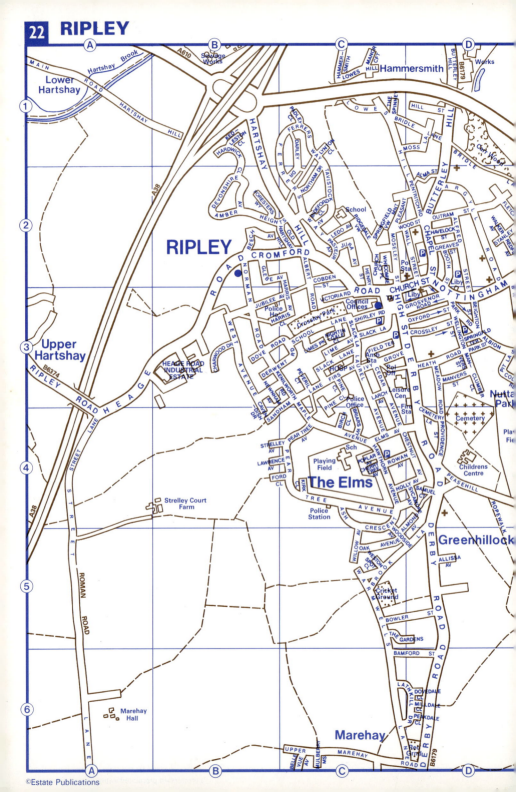

RIPLEY

Lower Hartshay

Upper Hartshay

Hammersmith

Sewage Works

Works

HEAGE ROAD INDUSTRIAL ESTATE

Strelley Court Farm

The Elms

Police Station

Greenhillock

Childrens Centre

Cemetery

Nutta Park

Cricket Ground

The Gardens

Marehay Hall

Marehay

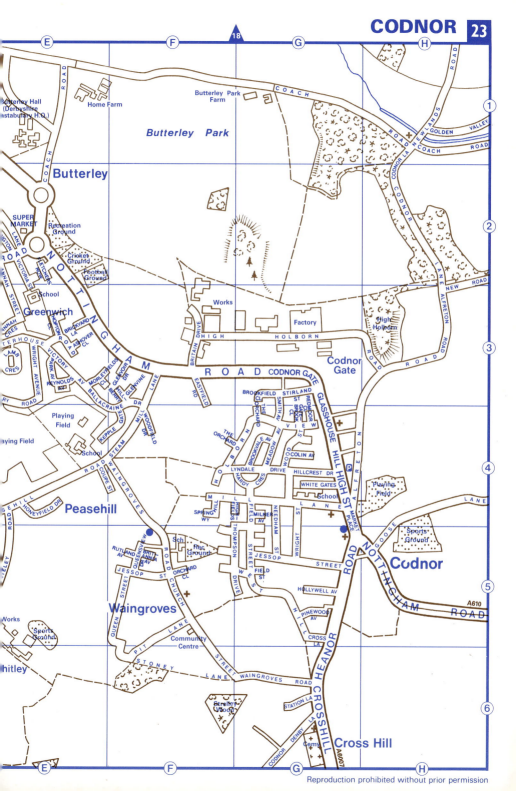

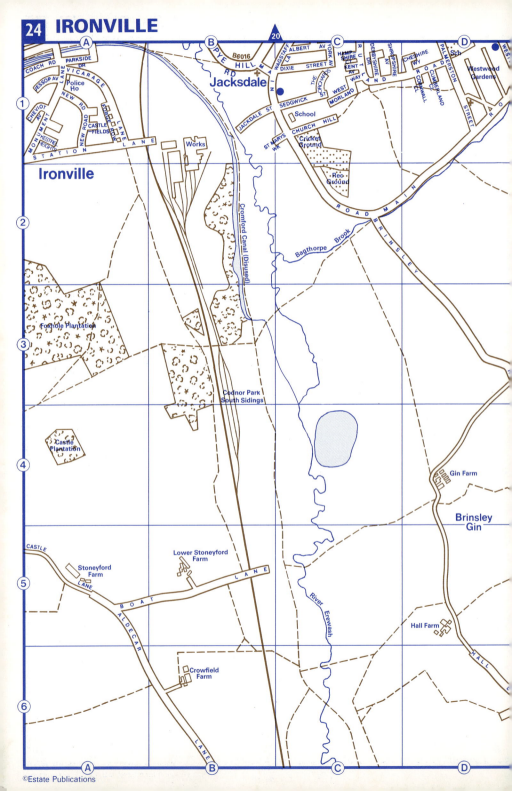

Jacksdale

Ironville

Cromford Canal (Disused)

Bagthorpe Brook

BRINSLEY

ROAD MAIN

Works

School

St Marys Wk

Cricket Ground

Rec Ground

CHURCH HILL

SEDGWICK

JACKDALE ST

MORLAND

WEST

B6016

PYE HILL

DIXIE STREET

ALBERT AV

WAGSTAFF LA

YORK AV

HAMPSHIRE AV

KENT AV

DERBYSHIRE AV

SHROPSHIRE

CHESHIRE WY

CUMBERLAND CL

CORNWALL

PALMERSTON

Sch

Westwood Gardens

STREET

THE POPLARS

WAY

ROAD

COACH RD

PARKSIDE DR

VICARAGE RD

JESSOP AV

NEW RD

Police Ho

CHEVIOT AV

KESTREL HEIGHTS

MONUMENT

STATION

NEW ROAD

CASTLE FIELDS

CASTLE LANE

Foxhole Plantation

Castle Plantation

Codnor Park South Sidings

Gin Farm

Brinsley Gin

CASTLE LANE

Stoneyford Farm

Lower Stoneyford Farm

LANE

BOAT LANE

ALDERCAR

River Erewash

Hall Farm

HALL

Crowfield Farm

LANE

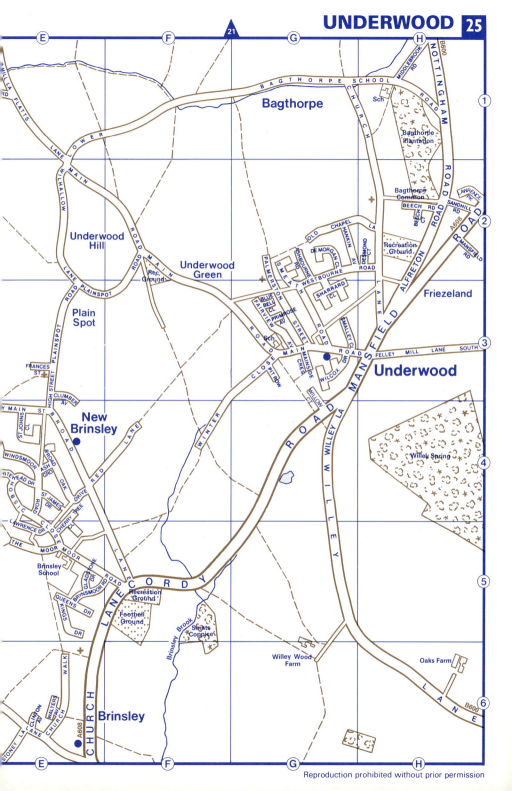

E   F   21   G   H

B600

MIDDLEBROOK RD

1

NOTTINGHAM ROAD

Bagthorpe

BAGTHORPE SCHOOL CHURCH

Sch

Bagthorpe Plantation

Bagthorpe Common

LAWRENCE PK

BEECH RD   SANDHILL RD

A608

MANSFIELD RD

2

BEECH CT

ALFRETON ROAD

MILLA FLATTS RD

LANE LOWER MAIN WILMALLOW

Underwood Hill

ROAD MAIN

ROAD PLAINSPOT

Rec. Ground

Underwood Green

OLD HANKIN AV   CHAPEL LA

DE MORGAN CL   DESMOND ROAD

PALMERSTON   ASHBOURNE RD   SMEATH   WESTBOURNE   MAINSIDE LANE

Recreation Ground

Friezeland

Plain Spot

LANE PLAINSPOT

BLUE BELL CL   FAIRVIEW   PRIMROSE AV

SHARRARD CL

SMALLEY CL

3

FRANCES ST

HIGH STREET

CLUMBER AV

ROAD   CLOSE PITROW   MAIN STREET   MAINSIDE CRES   ROAD

SCH

WILCOX

FELLEY   MILL   LANE   SOUTH

Underwood

MANSFIELD ROAD

Y MAIN ST   ST JOHNS CL

BROAD   ROAD RED   LANE

New Brinsley

WINTER

WILLOW CT

WILLEY LA

WILLEY

4

Willey Spring

WINDSMOOR   ASH GRO   BROAD OAK

WHITEHEAD DR   ST JAMES DR   CHERRY TREE CL   DRIVE

ROBSIC ROAD

LAWRENCE CLOSE

THE MOOR   MOOR

GLADSTONE DR

BRYNSMOOR RD

ROAD

CORDY

LANE

5

Brinsley School

QUEENS DR   KINGS DR

Recreation Ground

Football Ground

Brinsley Brook

Saints Coppice

Willey Wood Farm

Oaks Farm

B600

6

STONEY LA   CLINTON AV   WALTERS AV

WALK

CHURCH LANE   CHURCH LANE

Brinsley

A608

E   F   G   H

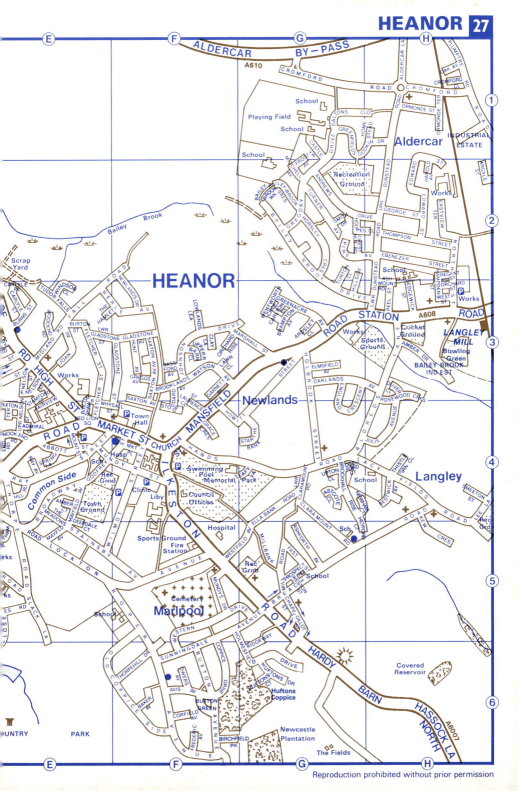

ALDERCAR BY-PASS

A610

HEANOR

Bailey Brook

Aldercar

Langley Mill

Newlands

Langley

Common Side

Marlpool

Country Park

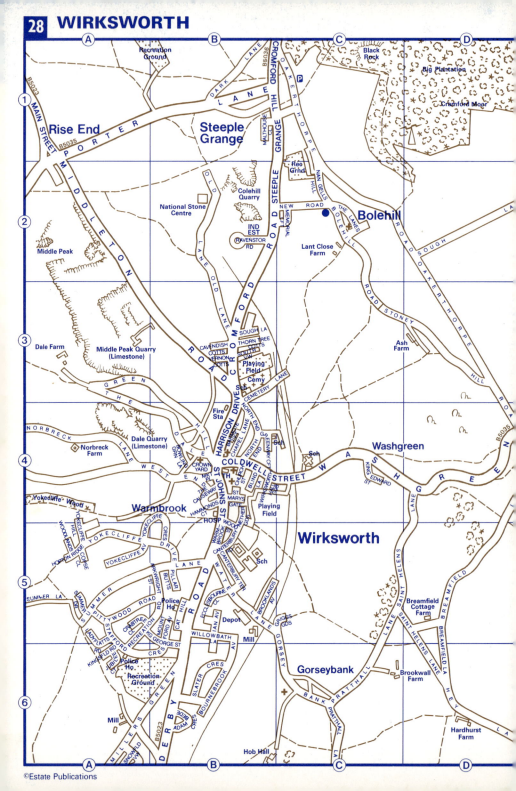

Recreation Ground

Rise End

Steeple Grange

Black Rock

Big Plantation

Cranford Moor

B5023

MAIN STREET

B5035

PORTER

LANE

DARK LANE

CROMFORD HILL

B5035

OAKERTHORPE

MIDDLETON

National Stone Centre

Colehill Quarry

OLD LANE

STEEPLE GRANGE

Rec Grnd

NEW ROAD

MEMORIAL

NAN GELLS HILL

THE LANES

BOLEHILL

Bolehill

Middle Peak

IND EST

RAVENSTOR RD

Lant Close Farm

ROAD

SOUGH

OAKERTHORPE ROAD

Dale Farm

Middle Peak Quarry (Limestone)

CROMFORD ROAD

OLD LANE

DALE LANE

SOUGH LA

CAVENDISH COTTS

VERNON COTTS

THORN TREE COTTS

SOUGH JW

Playing Field

Cemy

Sch

Fire Sta

ROAD STONEY

Ash Farm

HILL ROAD

THE GREEN

NORBRECK

Norbreck Farm

Dale Quarry (Limestone)

WEST END

HARRISON DRIVE

GREEN HILL

NORTH END

CHAPEL LANE

NORTH ST

CEMETERY LANE

GREENWAY LANE

Sch

Sch

Washgreen

WASHGREEN

KING EDWARD ST

Yokecliffe Wood

Warmbrook

YOKECLIFFE HILL

WOODLANDS

HOPTON RIDGE CLOSE

YOKECLIFFE AV

YOKECLIFFE AV

YOKECLIFFE CRES

DRIVE

ST JOHNS ST

CROWN YARD

THE CAUSEWAY

ST MARYS GATE

NETHER

COLDWELL STREET

BLIND LANE

HOSP

HAMMONDS

WOOD

CT

WATER LANE

BROOK

CANTERBURY TER

Playing Field

Sch

Wirksworth

SAINT HELENS LANE

BREAMFIELD

Breamfield Cottage Farm

BREAMFIELD LA

HEY

SUMMER LA

SUMMER RD

PITTYWOOD ROAD

RECREATION RD

MOUNT FORD RD

KG GEORGE ST

CENTRE CL

STAFFORD

LADY FLATTS RD

KINGFIELD RD

JUBILEE

Police Ho.

Recreation Ground

ARKWRIGHT ST

CAT TAIL

BUTTS

PILLAR

DERBY ROAD

ECCLESBOURNE AV

ST

JULIAN AV

Police Ho.

Depot

WILLOWBATH LANE

Mill

SLATER CRES

GREEN

BOURNEBROOK

CRES

ADAM BEDE CRES

BROOKLANDS AV

GORSEY LANE

GRIGG GDS

Gorseybank

BANK

PRATTHALL

PRATTHALL LA

SAINT HELENS LANE

Brookwall Farm

BREAMFIELD LA

HEY

Mill

Hob Hall

Hardhurst Farm

A - Z INDEX TO STREETS
with Postcodes

he Index includes some
ames for which there is
isufficient space on the
haps. These names are
receded by an * and are
ollowed by the nearest
djoining thoroughfare.

Abbey Clo. DE55 — 16 B3
Abbots Gro. DE56 — 10 B3
Abbott Rd. DE55 — 15 E5
Abbott St. DE75 — 27 E4
Accomodation
  Rd. NG16 — 20 A6
Acer Clo. DE16 — 16 C5
Acorn Dri. DE56 — 10 C3
Acorn Ridge. DE4 — 4 C2
Acorn Way,
  Acorn Dri. DE56 — 10 C3
Acdale Rd. DE75 — 26 C5
Adam Bede Cres. DE4 — 28 B6
Adams Clo. DE75 — 26 D6
Addison St. DE55 — 15 E4
Addison Sq. DE4 — 6 B6
Addison St. DE55 — 12 D2
Adelaide Wk,
  Regent Clo. NG16 — 19 H6
Admiral Clo. DE75 — 27 E4
Alabaster La. DE4 — 6 B5
Albert Av. NG16 — 20 B6
Albert Rd. DE5 — 22 C2
Albert St, Belper. DE56 — 10 B4
Albert St,
  Ironville. NG16 — 19 H5
Albert St,
  Somercotes. DE55 — 19 E2
Albert St, Sth
  Normanton. DE55 — 16 B1
Alberta Av. NG16 — 21 G3
Albion St. DE5 — 22 D3
Aldecar La. NG16 — 24 A5
Alder Rd. DE56 — 11 C5
Aldercar By-Pass. NG16 — 27 F1
Aldercar La. NG16 — 27 H1
Alders La. DE4 — 5 H6
Aldreds La. DE75 — 27 G4
Alexander Av. NG16 — 21 E3
Alexander Ter. DE16 — 16 D6
Alfred St,
  Alfreton. DE55 — 14 C5
Alfred St,
  Pinxton. DE16 — 16 D4
Alfred St,
  Riddings. DE55 — 19 F4
Alfred St, Ripley. DE5 — 22 D2
Alfred St, Sth
  Normanton. DE55 — 15 H3
Alfreton By-Pass. DE55 — 14 B6
Alfreton Rd. DE55 — 17 F1
Alfreton Rd,
  Codnor. DE5 — 23 G4
Alfreton Rd,
  Matlock.DE4 — 5 E5
Alfreton Rd,
  Pinxton. NG16 — 16 C3
Alfreton Rd,
  Primrose Hill. DE55 — 13 A8
Alfreton Rd,
  Selston Grn. NG16 — 20 B4
Alfreton Rd, Sth
  Normanton. DE55 — 15 H3
Alfreton Rd,
  Tibshelf. DE55 — 12 B4
Alfreton Rd,
  Underwood. NG16 — 25 H2
All Saints Rd. DE4 — 4 C3
Allan Dale Rd. DE75 — 27 E3
Allen A Dale Rd. NG16 — 21 H3
Allen Hill. DE4 — 4 C3
Allens Green Av. NG16 — 21 F4
Allissa Av. DE5 — 22 D5
Allstone Lee. DE56 — 10 B3
Alma Rd. NG16 — 21 G5
Alma St. DE5 — 22 D2
Alma St. DE5 — 14 D4
Almond Av. DE5 — 22 C5
Almond Gro. DE56 — 18 D2
Alport Clo. DE56 — 10 D2
Althorp Clo. DE55 — 18 C3
Alton Rise. DE4 — 4 A2
Alton Road. DE56 — 10 C1
Alverton Ct. DE56 — 10 C1

Amber Ct. DE75 — 27 E4
Amber Dri. NG16 — 27 H3
Amber Gro. DE55 — 14 C5
Amber Heights. DE5 — 22 B2
Amber Rd. DE56 — 9 E6
Amber View Rd. DE56 — 9 E5
Amberdene. DE4 — 5 E3
Amecroft La. DE4 — 4 B1
Andrews Dri. NG16 — 27 G2
Annesley La. NG16 — 21 G4
Appleton Dri. DE56 — 10 D2
Applewood Clo. DE56 — 10 D2
Ardsley Clo. DE75 — 27 G3
Arran Ct. DE55 — 12 C3
Argyll Rd. DE5 — 22 D3
Arkwright Av. DE56 — 10 E2
Arkwright St. DE4 — 28 B5
Arlington St. DE55 — 18 B3
Arran Ct. DE55 — 12 C3
Arthur St. DE16 — 16 D4
Arthur St. DE55 — 14 C3
Ash Acre. DE56 — 10 F3
Ash Clo. DE16 — 16 D5
Ash Cres. DE5 — 22 C4
Ash Gro,
  New Brinsley. NG16 — 25 E4
Ash Gro,
  Selston. NG16 — 21 F3
Ashbourne Rd. NG16 — 25 G2
Ashfield Av. DE55 — 19 F1
Ashford Rise. DE56 — 10 D2
Ashforth Av. DE75 — 27 G5
Ashley Clo. DE4 — 5 H5
Ashmount Rd. DE75 — 27 H3
Ashop Rd. DE56 — 10 F3
Ashover Clo. DE55 — 23 E3
Ashton Clo. DE55 — 18 C3
Ashton Way. DE56 — 10 F3
Asker La. DE4 — 5 E3
Astcote Clo. DE75 — 27 G4
Avis Av. DE75 — 27 F6
Azalea Av. DE55 — 18 C2
Azalea Clo. DE55 — 15 G5

Babbington St. DE55 — 12 D3
Back La. DE55 — 12 C3
Bailey Brook
  Cres. NG16 — 27 G2
Bailey Brook Dri. NG16 — 27 G2
Bailey Brook Wk. NG16 — 27 G2
Baker Av. NG16 — 20 C6
Baker Av. DE75 — 27 F6
Baker Clo. DE55 — 19 F3
Bakers La. DE4 — 6 B6
Bakewell Rd. DE4 — 4 A1
Ball Hill. DE4 — 16 C2
Ballacraine Dri. DE55 — 23 E3
Bamford St. DE5 — 22 C6
Bamford St. DE55 — 13 D5
Bank Clo. DE55 — 12 C4
Bank Rd. DE4 — 4 D3
Bank St. DE55 — 19 F2
Banks Burn Clo. DE75 — 26 D4
Bargate Clo. DE56 — 11 E6
Bargate Rd. DE56 — 11 C5
Barley Cft. DE55 — 16 B3
Barmote Cft. DE4 — 28 B4
Barnwell La. DE4 — 6 B6
Barrows Hill La. NG16 — 20 D5
Barton Knowle. DE56 — 10 E3
Bassford Av. DE75 — 27 F3
Beaufit La. NG16 — 18 E5
Beaulieu Way. DE55 — 18 C2
Beaumont Clo. DE56 — 10 F3
Beaurepaire Cres. DE56 — 10 D2
Becksitch La. DE56 — 11 B5
Bedehouse La. DE4 — 6 C6
Beech Av. DE5 — 22 B2
Beech Av. DE5 — 14 D3
Beech Av. NG16 — 17 E5
Beech Ct. NG16 — 25 H2
Beech Gro. DE56 — 16 B3
Beech Rd. NG16 — 25 H2
Beechwood Clo. DE56 — 10 A2
Beighton St. DE5 — 22 D3
Belfield Ct. DE75 — 26 C1
Belgrave Clo. DE56 — 10 E2
Belle Acre Clo. DE56 — 10 B4
Belle Vue Av. DE5 — 22 C5
Belper La. DE56 — 10 A1
Belper Rd. DE56 — 11 E6

Belvedere Clo. DE55 — 18 C3
Belvoir Way. DE55 — 19 E1
Bent La. DE4 — 4 D2
Bentley Clo. DE4 — 5 E2
Bentley Clo. DE4 — 15 D4
Berle Av. DE75 — 27 E3
Berristow La. DE55 — 13 F8
Bessalone Dri. DE56 — 10 C2
Bestwick Av. DE75 — 27 H4
Bestwood Rd. NG16 — 17 E5
Bideford Clo. DE55 — 22 C2
Bidston Clo. DE4 — 4 D2
Billingsley Av. DE16 — 16 D6
Birch Clo. DE5 — 22 C4
Birch Clo. DE55 — 14 D3
Birch Vale. DE56 — 10 B2
Birchen Holme. DE56 — 16 A4
Birchwood Clo. DE55 — 16 B4
Birchwood Cres. DE55 — 19 F2
Birchwood La. DE55 — 15 H3
Birchwood Rd. DE55 — 15 E5
Birchwood Way. DE55 — 15 E6
Bircumshaw Rd. DE75 — 27 E4
Bishop St. DE55 — 14 C3
Blackrocks Av. DE4 — 4 A2
Blackstone Clo — 19 F3
Blind La. DE4 — 28 B4
Blisworth Way. DE55 — 18 B3
Bloomfield Rd. DE55 — 18 C2
Blue Bell Clo,
  Selston. NG16 — 21 H3
Blue Bell Clo,
  Underwood. NG16 — 25 G3
Bluebell Clo. DE55 — 15 G5
Boam La. DE4 — 4 B1
Boat La. NG16 — 24 A5
Bobbin Mill Hill. DE56 — 9 E5
Bolehill Rd. DE4 — 28 C2
Bolton St. DE55 — 18 A3
Bonnington Dri. DE55 — 19 F2
Bonsall Dri. DE55 — 19 F2
Bonsall La. DE55 — 14 C4
Booth St. DE5 — 22 D2
*Bosley Mews,
  Abbotts Gro. DE56 — 10 C3
Boughton Dri. DE55 — 18 C2
Boundary Gdns. DE55 — 12 C4
Bourne Av. NG16 — 21 G2
Bournebrook Av. DE4 — 28 B6
Bowler St. DE5 — 22 C5
Bowling Grn La. DE4 — 28 B4
Bowmer La. DE56 — 9 E5
Bowns Hill. DE4 — 8 D3
Brackendale Rd. DE55 — 18 B2
Bradley Dri. DE56 — 10 F3
Bradshaw Av. DE55 — 19 G4
Bradshaw Croft. DE56 — 10 A2
Bradwell Way. DE56 — 10 D2
*Brafield Clo,
  Naseby Rd. DE56 — 10 F3
Bramble Way. DE55 — 16 B3
Bramley St. DE55 — 19 G3
Brampton Av. DE75 — 27 G3
Brampton Ct. DE55 — 10 F3
Braybrook Clo. DE55 — 18 C2
Breach Rd, Denby
  Common. DE75 — 26 A2
Breach Rd,
  Marlpool. DE75 — 27 F6
Breamfield La. DE4 — 28 D5
Brenden Av. DE55 — 19 E3
Brenden Clo. DE55 — 19 F2
Briar Clo. DE55 — 15 E5
Briars La. DE56 — 9 D5
Briars Way. DE5 — 22 C4
Brickyard La. DE55 — 23 E3
Brickyard La. DE56 — 16 A2
Bridge End Av. NG16 — 21 G2
Bridge Foot. DE56 — 10 B3
Bridge Hill. DE56 — 10 A3
Bridge St. DE56 — 10 B3
Bridge View. DE56 — 11 C8
Bridle La. DE55 — 22 C1
Bridle La. DE5 — 23 E5
Bright St. DE55 — 16 A3
Brinsley Hill. DE75 — 24 D1
Britain Dri. DE55 — 23 F3
Britannia Av. DE5 — 23 F5
Broad La. NG16 — 25 E4
Broad Oak Dri. NG16 — 25 E4
Broadlands. DE56 — 16 A4
Broadway. DE55 — 22 D3
Broadway. DE55 — 18 B3

Broadway. DE75 — 27 E4
Brockhall Rise. DE75 — 27 G4
Brook Av. DE55 — 14 D5
Brook Clo. DE55 — 14 D5
Brook La. DE5 — 22 C5
Brook La. DE55 — 14 D5
Brook St. DE75 — 26 C1
Brooke St. DE55 — 12 D2
Brookfield Clo. DE5 — 23 G3
Brookfield Way. DE4 — 5 G5
Brookhill Av. NG16 — 17 E4
Brookhill La. DE16 — 16 D4
Brooklands Av. DE4 — 28 B5
Brooklands Av. DE5 — 23 G4
Brookside. DE56 — 10 B4
Brookvale Av. DE5 — 23 G4
Broom Acre.DE55 — 16 C4
Broom Av. DE55 — 18 C3
Broom Clo. DE56 — 10 A2
Broome Av. DE75 — 26 C2
Browns La. DE56 — 11 F8
Brunswood Rd. DE4 — 6 C1
Brynsmoor Rd. NG16 — 25 E5
Buckfast Clo. DE55 — 18 B2
Buckingham Clo. DE55 — 18 C3
Bull La. DE5 — 5 F3
Bullbridge Hill. DE56 — 9 E6
Bulling La. DE4 — 8 C3
Bullock La. DE55 — 19 G5
Bullsmore. DE56 — 10 E3
Bunyan Green
  Rd. NG16 — 20 D3
Burbage Clo. DE56 — 10 D2
Burke Dri. DE55 — 19 F2
Burleigh Cres. DE55 — 18 B2
Burnett La. DE4 — 4 B1
Burns St. DE75 — 27 E3
Burnthouse Rd. DE75 — 26 D4
Burton St. DE75 — 27 E3
Butterfield Cres. DE55 — 18 B3
Butterley Hill. DE5 — 22 D1
Butterley La. DE56 — 18 A6
Butts Dri. DE4 — 5 E5
Buxton Av. DE56 — 27 F6
Buxton Grn. DE75 — 27 F6
Byron Av. DE55 — 15 E4

*Cadeby Ct,
  Cantley Rd. DE55 — 19 F4
Caernarvon Clo. DE55 — 18 C3
Calladine Clo. DE75 — 26 D3
Calver Clo. DE56 — 10 D2
Cambridge St. DE55 — 13 B7
Campbell St. DE56 — 10 B4
Canada St. DE56 — 11 C5
Canterbury Rd. DE4 — 28 B5
Canterbury Ter. DE4 — 28 B5
Cantley Rd. DE55 — 19 F4
Carlton Clo. DE75 — 27 G3
Carlyle Pl. DE75 — 27 E3
Carlyle St. DE75 — 27 E3
Carnfield Hill. DE55 — 15 E3
Carnham Clo. DE55 — 15 F6
Carr Clo. DE55 — 16 A1
Carr La. DE4 — 7 E1
Carr La. DE55 — 16 A1
Carson Croft. DE4 — 4 D3
Carter La East. DE55 — 16 D2
Carter La West. DE55 — 16 C3
Casson St. NG16 — 19 H6
Castle Dri. DE55 — 19 F2
Castle Fields. NG16 — 24 A1
Castle La. NG16 — 24 A5
Castle View. NG16 — 27 G1
Castle View Dri. DE4 — 6 D6
Castleton Av. DE55 — 19 E4
Castleton Clo. NG16 — 21 G3
Cat Hill. DE4 — 28 B5
Catherine St. DE55 — 15 E3
Causeway La. DE4 — 4 D4
Cavendish Cotts. DE4 — 28 B3
Cavendish Dri. DE56 — 22 B3
Cavendish Rd. DE4 — 4 D2
Cedar Av. DE55 — 22 C3
Cedar Av. DE55 — 14 D3
*Cedar Dri,
  Manitoba Way. NG16 — 21 F3
Cedar Gro. DE55 — 16 B4
Cedar Gro. DE5 — 11 D5
Cemetery La. DE4 — 28 B3
Cemetery La. DE5 — 22 D4

Cemetery Rd. DE55 — 19 E3
Cemetery Rd. DE56 — 10 C2
Central Av. DE55 — 16 B2
Central Dri. . DE55 — 13 B7
Central Av. DE55 — 14 C4
Chadwick Nick La. DE56 — 8 C4
Chapel Hill. DE5 — 6 B5
Chapel La, Crich. DE4 — 8 D3
Chapel La,
  Wirksworth. DE4 — 28 B4
Chapel Rd. NG16 — 21 F4
Chapel St,
  Alfreton. DE55 — 14 C4
Chapel St, Belper. DE56 — 10 B4
Chapel St,
  Fritchley. DE56 — 9 E5
Chapel St,
  Holbrook Moor. DE56 — 11 E8
Chapel St,
  Marlpool. DE75 — 27 G5
Chapel St, Ripley. DE5 — 22 D2
Chapel St,
  Selston. NG16 — 21 G3
Chapel St,
  Somercotes. DE55 — 19 E3
Chapel St,
  Swanwick. DE55 — 18 B3
Charity Rd. DE55 — 19 E4
Charles St,
  Alfreton. DE55 — 14 C3
Charles St,
  Somercotes. DE55 — 19 E3
Charnwood Av. DE56 — 10 C3
Charnwood Clo. DE55 — 18 C3
Charnwood Cres. DE55 — 13 E5
Charwood Dri. DE5 — 22 B3
Chase Rd. DE56 — 9 C7
Chase View. DE4 — 8 C3
Chatham Av. DE55 — 15 E5
Chatsworth Av,
  Crich. DE4 — 8 C3
Chatsworth Av,
  Matlock. DE4 — 4 A2
Chatsworth Av,
  Selston. NG16 — 21 G3
Chatsworth Clo. DE55 — 14 C4
Chatsworth St. DE55 — 12 D3
Cheapside. DE56 — 10 B4
Cherry Clo. DE55 — 16 B1
Cherry Tree Av. DE5 — 22 C4
Cherry Tree Clo. DE55 — 18 D3
Cherry Tree Rd. NG16 — 10 D1
Cherry Tree Clo. NG16 — 25 E5
Cheshire Way. NG16 — 20 C6
Chesterfield Rd,
  Alfreton. DE55 — 14 B1
Chestorfield Rd,
  Belper. DE56 — 10 C3
Chesterfield Rd,
  Far Laund. DE56 — 10 E1
Chesterfield Rd,
  Lane End. DE56 — 12 D1
Chesterfield Rd,
  Matlock. DE4 — 5 E4
Chestnut Av,
  Cowhill. DE56 — 11 C5
Chestnut Av,
  Holbrook Moor. DE56 — 11 E8
Chestnut Av,
  Riddings. DE55 — 19 F5
Chestnut Av,
  Ripley. DE5 — 22 D4
Chestnut Bank. DE75 — 26 D4
Chestnut Dri. DE55 — 16 B3
*Chestnut Dri,
  Manitoba Way. NG16 — 21 F3
Chestnut Gro. DE55 — 12 C4
Chestnut Rd. DE75 — 27 G2
Chestnut Way. DE55 — 18 C2
Chevin Rd. DE56 — 11 A5
Cheviot Av. NG16 — 24 A1
Church Croft. DE5 — 22 C2
Church Hill,
  Blackwell. DE55 — 13 D7
Church Hill,
  Jacksdale. NG16 — 24 C1
Church La,
  Bagthorpe. NG16 — 25 G1
Church La,
  Belper. DE56 — 10 C4
Church La,
  Brinsley. NG16 — 25 E6
Church La,
  Selston Grn. NG16 — 20 D3

Entry	Ref
Church La, Tibshelf. DE55	12 C2
Church St, Alfreton. DE55	14 C4
Church St, Frithley. DE16	9 E5
Church St, Heanor. DE75	27 F4
Church St, Holloway. DE4	7 H4
Church St, Matlock. DE4	4 D5
Church St, Riddings. DE55	19 F4
Church St, Ripley. DE5	22 C3
Church St, Sth Normanton. DE55	16 B1
Church St, Tansley Knoll. DE4	5 H4
Church St, Waingroves. DE5	23 F5
Church St, Wirksworth. DE4	28 B4
Church St East. NG55	17 E4
Church St West. NG16	16 D5
Church Vw. DE75	26 C2
Church Walk. NG16	25 E6
Cinder Bank. NG16	19 H6
Cinder Rd. DE55	19 G3
Claramount Rd. DE75	27 G4
Clarke Av. DE75	26 D3
Clatterway. DE4	6 A4
Claxton St. DE75	27 E4
Claxton Ter. DE75	27 E4
Clayton Gro. DE75	26 D1
Cleve Av. DE4	4 B2
Cliff La. NG16	17 G4
Cliff Nook. DE55	16 C4
Clifton Rd. DE4	6 B3
Clinton Av. NG16	25 E6
Clover Nook La. DE55	15 G5
Clover Nook Rd. DE55	15 F6
Clumber Av. NG16	25 E3
Clumber Clo. DE5	22 D3
Cluster Rd. DE56	10 B3
Coach Rd. NG16	23 E2
Coast Hill. DE4	8 C2
Cobden St. DE55S	22 C2
Cockshutt La. DE55	19 H2
Codnor-Denby La. DE75	26 A1
Codnor Denby La. DE5	23 G6
Codnor Gate. DE5	23 G3
Codnor La. NG16	23 H2
Coldwell St. DE4	28 B4
Colin Av. DE5	23 G4
Colin St. DE55	14 D4
Colledge St. DE55	19 F4
Colliery Rd, Alfreton. DE55	14 B5
Colliery Rd, Blackwell. DE55	13 C7
Colliery Rd, Pinxton. NG16	17 E5
Colliery Rd, Ripley. DE5	22 D3
Collingwood Cres. DE4	4 B3
Collins Av. DE55	16 B1
Columbia Clo. NG16	21 G3
Common Side. NG16	21 F2
Connaught Ct. DE55	14 D4
Coppice Dri. DE75	27 F6
Coppice View. DE55	16 A4
Copse Clo. DE4	28 A5
Copse Wood. DE55	16 A4
Cordy Rd. NG16	25 F5
Corfield Av. DE75	27 F6
Corn Clo. DE55	16 C2
Corn Dri. DE55	16 C2
Cornfield Av. DE55	16 A4
Cornhill Dri. DE55	14 D4
Cornwall Clo. NG16	20 C6
Coronation Av. DE56	10 C2
Coronation Dri. DE56	16 B3
Cotes Park La. DE55	15 E6
Cottage Gdns. DE75	26 D3
Coupe St. DE5	23 E4
Coupland Pl. DE55	19 E2
Courtney Way. DE56	10 F3
Cowham Clo. DE5	15 E4
Crabtree Clo. DE4	28 A5
Cragg La. DE55	13 D6
Crays Hill. DE55	18 D3
Crescent Rd. NG16	20 D4
Cressy Rd. DE5	14 C4
Crich La, Belper. DE56	10 C1
Crich La, Bullbridge. DE56	9 E8
Crich Rd. DE56	9 D5
Crich View. DE55	13 D5
Croft Clo. NG16	16 C4
Cromford Clo. NG16	27 H1
Cromford Hill, Cromford. DE4	6 B6
Cromford Hill, Wirksworth. DE4	28 B1
Cromford Rd, Aldercar. NG16	27 G1
Cromford Rd, Crich. DE4	8 C2
Cromford Rd, Ripley. DE5	22 B2
Cromford Rd, Wirksworth. DE4	28 B3
Cromwell Av. DE55	13 B8
Cromwell Dri. DE55	18 A3
Crook Stile. DE4	4 C2
Cross La. DE5	23 G5
Crosshill. DE55	23 G6
Crossley St. DE5	22 D3
Crown Sq. DE4	4 C4
Crown Yard. DE4	28 B4
Culland View. DE4	8 D3
Culworth Clo. DE56	10 F3
Cumberland Clo. NG16	20 C6
Cunnery La. DE4	7 H1
Cutt St. NG16	17 E5
Dahlia Av. DE55	16 B1
Dale Av, Riddings. DE55	19 E4
Dale Av, Newton. DE55	13 D5
Dale Clo. DE56	9 D5
Dale Rd. DE4	4 C4
Dale Rd South. DE4	4 A1
Dales Field. DE4	4 B3
Dalewood Clo. DE55	16 A4
Daltons Clo. NG16	27 G1
Dannah Cres. DE5	23 E3
Dannah St. DE5	23 E2
Dark La, Milford. DE56	11 D8
Dark La, Wirksworth. DE4	28 B1
Darley Dri. DE5	22 C1
Darley House Est. DE4	4 A1
Days La. DE56	10 B4
Days Mill Clo. DE4	4 B3
De Morgan Clo. NG16	25 G2
Deacon Clo. DE55	18 B3
Deamon St. DE55	13 B8
Deep Carr La. DE4	5 E5
Deepdale. NG16	19 H6
Deepdale Ct. DE75	27 E4
Deepdale Rd. DE56	10 D3
Delamere Clo. NG16	18 B3
Delves Rd. DE75	26 D5
Denby Common. DE55	26 A3
Dene Fields Ct. DE4	4 D4
Denton Way. DE55	18 C3
Derby Rd, Alfreton. DE55	14 B5
Derby Rd, Ambergate. DE56	9 C8
Derby Rd, Cowhill. DE56	11 B5
Derby Rd, Cromford. DE4	6 C4
Derby Rd, Hammersmith. DE55	18 A6
Derby Rd, Heanor. DE75	26 D4
Derby Rd, Ripley. DE5	22 D3
Derby Rd, Wirksworth. DE4	28 B6
Derbyshire Dri. NG16	20 D6
Derwent Av. DE56	11 C7
Derwent Dri. NG16	21 G3
Derwent Dri. DE55	12 C3
Derwent Gro. DE55	14 C5
Derwent Rd. DE5	22 B3
Derwent St. DE56	10 B4
Desborough Rd. NG16	21 E3
Desmond Ct. NG16	25 H2
Devonshire Av. DE4	4 B2
Devonshire Av. DE55	22 B2
Devonshire Dri. DE55	19 E3
Dimple La. DE4	8 D3
Dimple Rd. DE4	4 C3
Dixie St. NG16	20 B6
Dodford Ct. DE75	27 G4
Doe Hill La. DE55	12 A4
Douglas Av. DE55	26 D3
Douglas Rd. DE55	19 F2
Dove Dri. NG16	21 G3
Dove Rd. DE5	22 B3
Dovedale Clo. DE55	22 D6
Dovedale Cres. DE56	10 D3
Downing St. DE55	16 B1
Drabbles Rd. DE4	4 C3
Draycott Clo. DE75	26 C1
Drovers Way. DE56	9 E6
Duke St. DE55	16 B2
Dumbles La. DE75	26 A3
Duncan Clo. DE56	10 D2
Dunsford Rd. DE55	14 D2
Dunsil Rd. NG16	17 E6
Eachwell La. DE55	14 B5
East Cres. DE56	11 E7
East Nelson St. DE75	27 E3
East Ter. DE56	11 C8
Eastfield Dri. DE55	16 B2
Eastfield Rd. DE55	23 F3
Eastview Ter. NG16	27 H2
Ebenezer St. NG16	24 H2
Ecclesbourne Clo. DE4	28 B5
Edale Way. DE56	10 C3
Edensor Way. DE56	10 C2
Edge Rd. DE4	4 C3
Edgefold Rd. DE4	4 D4
Edinburgh Ct. DE55	18 C3
Edward Av. NG16	20 B6
Edward St, Aldercar. NG16	27 H2
Edward St, Belper. DE56	10 C3
Edwinstowe Dri. NG16	21 H3
Egreaves Av. DE75	26 C1
Elder Clo. DE55	18 D2
Elizabeth Pk. NG16	19 H5
Ella Bank Rd. DE75	27 G4
Ellesmere Av. DE55	14 D4
Elm Av, Cowhill. DE56	11 D5
Elm Av, Matlock. DE4	4 B2
Elm Clo. DE55	16 D5
Elmhurst Av. DE55	16 A3
Elmhurst Clo. DE55	16 A3
Elms Av. DE5	22 C4
Elms Av. DE55	14 D3
Elms Clo. DE55	14 D3
Elmsfield Av. DE75	27 G3
Elmtree Av. NG16	21 F3
Ember La. DE4	6 A2
England Cres. DE75	27 G3
Erewash Rd. NG16	17 E6
Erica Dri. DE55	16 B1
Everest Dri. DE56	19 F2
Ewart La. DE55	14 B5
*Eyam Wk, Acorn Dri. DE56	10 C3
Fairfield Av. DE55	13 F8
Fairholmes. DE4S	4 A1
Fairview. DE75	27 E4
Fairview Av. NG16	25 G3
Falcons Rise. DE56	10 E2
Fall Rd. DE75	27 E3
Far Cross. DE4	4 D2
Far Green. DE4	4 C3
Far Laund. DE56	10 D2
Farley Hill. DE4	4 B1
Farm Clo. DE55	19 F2
Farm Clo. DE56	10 E3
Fast St. DE75	27 G5
Fearn Av. DE5	23 E3
Felley Mill La South. NG16	25 H3
Fellside. DE56	10 C3
Fen Clo. DE55	13 D5
Fern Bank Av. DE55	13 B7
Ferrers Way. DE5	22 C1
Field La. DE55	15 G1
Field La. DE56	10 B4
Field St. DE5	23 G4
Field Ter. DE5	22 C3
Findern Clo. DE56	10 D2
Firs Av. DE5	22 C3
Firs Av. DE55	14 D3
Firs Par. DE4	4 D4
Flamstead Av. DE75	26 C1
Flatts La. NG16	25 E1
Fleet Cres. DE56	11 B5
Fleet Park. DE56	10 C4
Fletcher St. DE5	22 D2
Fletcher St. DE75	27 E3
Fletchers Row. DE55	23 E2
Flowery Leys La. DE55	15 E1
Ford Av. DE75	26 C1
Ford La. DE55	22 B4
Ford St. DE56	10 C3
Fordbridge La. DE55	13 C7
Forest Clo. DE56	10 D2
Forest La. NG16	21 H3
Foresters Way. DE5	22 B2
Forge Row. NG16	24 A1
Fossetts Av. NG16	21 F3
Fox Croft. DE55	12 C4
Foxholes La. DE4	5 G2
Foxpark View. DE55	12 B4
Frances St. NG16	25 E3
Franklin Rd. NG16	20 B6
Fritchley La. DE75	27 F6
Frederick St. DE55	14 C3
Frederick St. DE55	19 F5
Friars Clo. NG16	21 H3
Fritchley La. DE56	9 E5
Froggatt Clo. DE55	19 F3
Front St. DE56	9 E5
Frost Av. NG16	27 G2
Furnace La. DE75	26 D1
Furnace Row. DE55	19 H3
Garden Cres. DE55	15 H3
Garner La. DE4	8 F2
Garnett Av. DE75	27 F3
Gatebrook Clo. DE55	23 G4
George Cres. DE55	19 E4
George Rd. DE4	5 E3
George St, Aldercar. NG16	27 H2
George St, Alfreton. DE55	14 D4
George St, Belper. DE56	10 B3
George St, Pinxton. DE55	16 C4
George St, Riddings. DE55	19 F4
George St, Somercotes. DE55	19 F2
George St, Sth Normanton. DE55	15 H3
Gibfield La. DE56	11 B5
Gill St. NG16	21 G4
Gilot St. DE75	27 G5
Gladstone Av. DE55	13 B8
Gladstone Av. DE75	27 F3
Gladstone Dri. NG16	25 E5
Gladstone St, Heanor. DE75	27 F3
Gladstone St, Sth Normanton. DE55	16 B2
Gladstone Ter. DE55	14 C5
Glasshouse Hill. DE56	23 G3
Glebe Av. NG16	17 E5
Glebe Av. DE5	22 B2
Glebe Clo. DE55	16 B3
Glen Av. DE56	11 E8
Glen Clo. DE55	13 D5
Glen Rd. DE4	8 A3
Glen View. DE56	11 C5
Glenvine. DE55	23 F3
Glenvoir Dri. DE5	23 F3
Glinton Av. DE55	13 B7
Gloves La. DE55	13 A6
Glue La. DE75	26 C3
Godfrey St. DE75	27 E4
Godkin Dri. NG16	27 G1
Golden Valley. DE55	23 H1
Golden Valley La. DE55	19 F6
Goldhill. DE4	5 H5
Goods Rd. DE56	11 B5
Gooker La. DE55	14 B5
Goose La. DE5	23 H5
Gordon Cres. DE55	16 B4
Gordon Rd. DE55	18 C2
Gorsey Rd. DE56	10 A2
Gorseybank. DE4	28 C5
Grace Cres. DE75	27 F4
Grammer St. DE75	26 B1
Grandfield St. DE55	26 D1
Grange Clo. DE55	15 H6
Grange St. DE55	14 C4
Grangewood Dri. DE56	11 C8
Gray Fallow. DE55	16 C4
Grayswood Clo. DE55	18 C3
Greaves St. DE5	22 D2
Green Clo. DE4	4 C3
Green Clo. DE55	13 D5
Green Cres. NG16	21 F4
Green Farm Rd. NG16	20 D3
Green Hill. DE58	28 A3
Green La. DE4	5 H4
Green La. DE56	10 B3
Green Sq Rd. NG16	17 E5
Greenacre Av. DE75	27 G3
Greenacres Dri. NG16	16 B1
Greenfields. DE55	22 D4
Greenhill Av. DE55	22 D4
Greenhill La. DE55	19 E3
Greenway Croft. DE4	28 B4
Greggs Av. DE75	27 F3
Gregory Dri. NG16	27 G2
Gregorys Way. DE56	10 F3
Grigg Gdns. DE4	28 C5
Gritstone Rd. DE4	5 E2
Grosvenor Rd. DE5	22 D3
Grove La. DE4	4 A
Grundy Av. NG16	21 E
Guildhall Dri. NG16	17 F
Hackney Rd. DE4	4 B
Haddon Clo. DE55	14 B
Haddon Clo. NG16	21 G
Haddon St. DE75	12 D
Hag La. DE56	9 E
Hall La. NG16	24 D
Hall La. DE55	13 D
Hall St. DE55	14 C
Hallfield Rd. DE55	13 D
Hallington Dri. DE75	26 D
Hamlet La. DE55	16 A
Hammer Leys. DE55	16 C
Hammersmith. DE5	22 C
Hammonds Ct. DE4	28 B
Hampden St. NG16	27 H
Hampshire Ct. NG16	20 C
Hands Rd. DE75	27 F
Hankin Av. NG16	25 G
Hanstubbin Rd. NG16	21 F
Hardie Av. DE55	16 A
Hardwick Clo. DE5	22 B
Hardwick Clo. DE55	13 A
Hardwick Dri. NG16	21 H
Hardwick St. DE55	12 D
Hardy Barn. DE75	27 G
Hardy Cres. DE5	23 G
Hardy St. DE55	14 C
Harold Av. NG16	27 H
Harpole Clo. DE55	18 C
Harrier Rd. DE56	10 E
Harris Av. DE5	22 C
Harris Clo. DE55	22 B
Harrison Dri. DE4	28 B
Harrison La. DE55	12 C
Hartingdon Dri. NG16	21 G
Hartshay Hill. DE5	22 A
Hasslewell Flat. DE56	16 C
Hassock La Nth. DE75	27 H
Haston Dri. DE55	19 F
Hathersage Dri. DE55	19 E
Havelock St. DE5	22 D
Hawkins Dri. DE56	9 E
Hawleys Clo. DE4	5 F
Hawthorn Av. DE5	22 C
Hawthorne Av. DE55	12 E
Hawthorne Dri. DE4	6 B
Hawthorne Rd. NG16	16 D
Hawthornes Av. DE55	15 H
Hayes. NG16	16 C
Hayes Cres. DE55	18 C
Hayes La. DE55	18 C
Hayfield Clo. DE56	10 D
Hazel Ct. DE75	26 D
Hazel Gro. DE55	5 E
Hazel Gro. DE55	16 C
Heage Rd. DE5	22 A
Heanor Gate Rd. DE75	26 D
Heanor Rd, Codnor. DE5	23 G
Heanor Rd, Denby Common. DE55	26 A
Heanor Rd, Heanor Gate. DE75	26 B
Heanor Rd, Loscoe. DE75	26 D
Hearthstone La. DE4	7 E
Heath Rd. DE55	22 D
Heather Clo, Sth Normanton. DE55	16 B
Heather Clo, Swanwick. DE55	18 C
Heathfield Gdns. DE55	12 D
Heathfield Rd. DE4	4 D
Hedley Clo. DE55	19 F
Henry Av. DE4	4 D
Henry Cres. DE55	15 E
Henry St. DE5	22 C
Hermitage Av. DE55	19 E
Hey La. DE4	28 C
Heydon Clo. DE56	10 D
Heyford St. DE75	27 G
Hickton Rd. DE55	18 E
*High Edge Mews, Acorn Dri. DE56	10 C
High Holborn Rd. DE5	23 F
High Pavement. DE56	10 C
High Ridge. DE4	4 D
High St, Alfreton. DE55	14 C
High St, Belper. DE56	10 C
High St, Codnor. DE5	23 C
High St, Heanor. DE75	27 E
High St, Loscoe. DE75	26 D
High St, New Brinsley. NG16	25 H
High St, Riddings. DE55	19 H

jh St, Ripley. DE5 22 C3
jh St, Somercotes. DE55 19 E2
jh St, Sth Normanton. DE55 16 A2
jh St, Swanwick. DE55 18 B3
jh St, Tibshelf. DE55 12 C4
jh View Rd. DE55 16 C1
jhfield Dri. DE4 5 E3
jhfield Dr. DE55 16 B3
jhfield Rd. DE55 18 A4
jhfield Rd. DE56 11 C5
jhfields. DE5 23 G4
jhwood Av. DE56 11 E6
cote La. DE55 13 C7
cote St. DE55 16 A1
l Crest. DE4 8 D2
l Fields. DE55 16 A4
l Rd. DE75 27 E4
l St. DE5 22 D1
l Top. DE56 9 E5
l Tops Vw. DE4 5 E4
lberry. DE5 23 F3
lcrest Av. DE55 16 A4
lcrest Dri. DE5 23 G4
lside, Heanor. NG16 27 G3
lside, Holloway. DE4 7 H5
lside Rise. DE56 11 B5
'top Rd. NG16 16 C4
top Rd. DE55 19 E5
ton Park Dri. DE55 19 E2
dersitch La. DE4 8 A3
bsic Clo. NG16 25 E4
bsic La. NG16 21 E1
ckley Way. DE55 14 D6
lborn View. DE5 23 F4
lbrook Rd. DE56 11 B5
lbrook St. DE75 27 G3
lland Cres. NG16 21 H3
lly Av. DE5 22 C4
lly Gro. DE55 18 C2
lly La. DE4 5 H5
lly La. DE56 9 A8
llyhead Rd. NG16 21 F4
llyhouse Dri. DE55 16 B1
llyhurst Ter. DE55 19 H4
llywell Av. DE5 23 G5
lme Clo. DE4 7 H6
lmes Clo. NG16 27 G2
lmes Rd. DE4 6 C2
lmes St. DE75 26 D3
lmesfield Clo. DE4 5 H4
lmesfield Dri. DE75 27 F5
lt Dri. DE4 4 B3
lt La. DE4 4 C4
me Farm Ct. NG16 20 D3
mecroft Dri. NG16 21 E2
mestead. NG16 27 H1
neyfield Dri. DE5 23 E4
oley St. NG16 21 F4
pe Ter. DE4 6 C1
pewell Rd. DE4 4 D3
pping Hill. DE56 11 B7
pton Clo. DE5 23 E3
pton Ridge. DE4 28 A5
rsley Cres. NG16 27 G2
rsley Cres. DE56 11 E8
rton Clo. DE55 18 C2
witt St. DE75 27 F4
nt Av. DE75 27 F3
nters Rd. DE56 10 F3
rds Hollow. DE4 4 B2
rker Rise. DE4 4 D2
rst Rise. DE4 5 E4
thwaite La. DE55 13 E7

Av. DE4 28 B5
ston Rd. DE75 27 F4
perial Rd. DE4 4 C3
ependent Hill. DE55 14 C5
DUSTRIAL ESTATES:
mber Business Ctr. DE55 19 E5
ailey Brook Ind Est. NG16 27 H3
rookhill Ind Est. NG16 17 E6
lover Nook Ind. Est. DE55 15 G5
otes Park Ind Est. DE55 15 F6
otes Park Ind Est West. DE55 19 F1
oods Rd Ind Est. DE56 11 B5
reenhill Ind Est. DE55 19 E4
eage Rd Ind Est. DE5 22 B3
...Nixs Hill Ind Est. DE55 14 D5
Inkerman Rd. NG16 21 F5
Inkerman St. NG16 21 F5
Institute La. DE55 14 C4
Intake La. DE4 6 C5
Iona Clo. DE55 12 C3
Ivy Gro. DE5 22 C3

Jackdale St. NG16 24 B1
Jackson Rd. DE4 4 C3
Jackson Tor Rd. DE4 4 C3
Jacksons La, Belper. DE56 10 F1
Jacksons La, Milford. DE56 11 A8
James St. DE55 19 E3
Jasmine Clo. DE55 18 C3
Jeffries La. DE4 8 C2
Jessop Av. NG16 24 A1
Jessop St, Codnor. DE5 23 G5
Jessop St, Waingroves. DE5 23 F5
Joan Av. DE75 27 E3
Jodrell Av. DE56 10 F4
John O'Gaunts Way. DE56 10 E3
John St, Alfreton. DE55 14 D4
John St, Matlock. DE4 4 C3
John St, Heanor. DE75 27 E3
John St, Somercotes. DE55 19 E2
Johns Pl. DE75 27 E4
Johnson Dri. DE75 27 F3
Joseph St. DE56 10 B3
Jubilee Av. DE5 22 B3
Jubilee Clo. DE4 28 A6
*Jubilee Ct, Kirkstead Clo. NG16 16 D5
Jubilee Ct. DE56 11 C5
Julie Av. DE75 27 H4
Jura Av. DE5 22 C2

Kedleston Clo. DE5 22 B1
Kedleston Ct. DE55 12 E3
Kenilworth Rd. DE5 22 B3
Kennack Clo. DE55 16 D1
Kent Av. NG16 20 C6
Kepple Gate. DE5 23 E4
Kestrel Heights. NG16 24 A1
Kew Cres. DE75 27 H4
Keys Rd. DE55 14 D5
Kilbourne Rd. DE56 10 E3
Kilburn La. DE56 10 F4
Killis La. DE56 11 F7
Kinder Cres. DE56 9 E6
King Edward St. DE4 28 C4
King George St. DE4 28 B5
King St, Alfreton. DE55 14 C5
King St, Belper. DE56 10 B4
King St, Lane End. DE55 12 D2
King St, Pinxton. NG16 16 D4
King St, Sth Normanton. DE55 16 A3
King William St. NG16 19 H6
Kings Dri. NG16 25 E5
Kings Way. DE75 27 E4
Kingsfield Rd. DE4 28 A6
Kingsway. DE75 26 D3
Kirk Clo. DE5 22 C4
Kirk La. DE56 10 D4
Kirkby La. NG16 17 G4
Kirkham Clo. DE75 27 E5
Kirkham La. DE56 9 E5
Kirkman Rd. DE75 26 C1
Kirkstead Clo. NG16 16 D5
Kirkstead Rd. NG16 16 D5
Kitson Av. NG16 20 C6
Knowle Av. DE56 10 A2
Knowlestone Pl. DE4 4 D5
Kynance Clo. DE55 16 D2

Laburnum Clo. DE55 16 B1
Laburnum Cres. DE55 18 C2
Lacy Fields Rd. DE75 27 G4
Ladyflatts Rd. DE4 28 A5
Ladywood Av. DE56 10 D2
Lake Av. DE75 26 D1
Lamb Cres. DE5 23 E3
Lambcroft Rd. NG16 16 D4
Lander La. DE56 10 C4
Langley Av. DE55 19 F2
Langton Hollow. NG16 20 D4
Lansbury Dri. DE55 16 A2
Larch Av. DE5 22 C3
Larchdale Clo. DE55 16 B4
Lark Hill. DE55 18 B2
Larkhill Clo. DE55 18 B2
Larkspur Clo. DE55 16 A4
Lathkil Dri. DE55 15 H3
Lathkil Gro. DE55 12 C3
Lathkill Dri. DE5 22 C6
Lathkill Dri. NG16 21 G3
Laund Av. DE56 10 D2
Laund Clo. DE56 10 D2
Laund Hill. DE56 10 C3
Laund Nook. DE56 10 D3
Laund Nook Rd. DE56 10 C3
Launds Av. NG16 21 E3
Laurel Av. DE5 22 C3
Laurel Clo. DE55 18 C2
Laurel Gro. DE55 16 A3
Lavender Rd. DE55 18 D2
Laverick Rd. NG16 20 B6
Lawn Clo. DE75 27 F3
Lawrence Av. DE5 22 B4
Lawrence Dri. NG16 25 E5
Lawrence Park. NG16 25 H2
Lea Bank. DE55 16 B4
Lea Cres. DE55 19 E4
Lea La. NG16 21 F4
Lea Rd. DE4 6 D4
Lea Vale. DE55 16 A4
Leabrooks Rd. DE55 19 E2
Leadale Av. DE55 18 D3
Leafy La. DE75 27 G4
Leamington Dri. DE55 16 B3
Leamington St. DE5 23 E2
Leamoor Av. DE55 19 E2
Leche Croft. DE56 10 F3
Ledo Av. DE5 22 C2
Lee La. DE75 27 H4
Lees La. DE55 15 G2
Leniscar Av. DE75 26 C2
Ley Av. DE55 15 E4
Ley Gdns. DE55 15 E4
*Leycote Way, Allstone Lee. DE56 10 B3
Lilac Ct. DE55 16 A3
Lilac Gro. DE55 16 A3
Lily Bank Clo. DE4 4 D4
Lime Av. DE5 22 C3
Lime Clo. NG16 16 D5
Lime Cres. DE56 11 D5
Lime Gro. DE55 16 B3
Lime Grove Av. DE4 4 D4
Lime Grove Walk. DE4 4 D4
Lime Tree Rd. DE4 4 D5
Limes Av. DE55 14 C4
Limes Park. DE5 22 C3
Lincoln Clo. DE55 12 D2
Lincoln St, Alfreton. DE55 14 C4
Lincoln St, Lane End. DE55 12 D2
Linden Gro. DE4 5 E4
Lindley St. NG16 21 E4
Little Breck. DE55 16 B4
Little Fen. DE55 12 C4
Little London. DE4 7 H6
Littlemoor La. DE4 7 F1
Littlemoor La. DE55 13 D5
Litton Clo. DE56 10 D3
Lockton Av. DE75 27 E5
Lodge Dri. DE56 10 A2
Long La. DE4 7 H4
Long Meadow Clo. DE55 14 C5
Long Meadow Rd. DE55 14 B5
Long Row. DE56 10 B3
Long Sleets. DE55 16 C4
Longload La. DE4 6 A6
Longstone Rise. DE56 10 D1
Longwood Rd. NG16 17 E5
Lonsdale Gro. DE4 4 A2
Loscoe - Denby La. DE75 26 B2
Loscoe Grange. DE75 26 D2
Loscoe Rd. DE75 27 E3
Love La. DE55 13 A6
Lower Bagthorpe. NG16 25 E1
Lower Claramount Rd. DE75 27 G4
Lower Dri. DE55 18 A3
Lower Dunstead Rd. NG16 27 H3
Lower Gladstone St. DE75 27 E3
Lower Somercotes. DE55 19 G3
Lowes Hill. DE5 22 C1
Lowlands Rd. DE56 10 D3
Lumsdale. DE4 5 F2
Lumsdale Cres. DE4 5 E4
Lumsdale Rd. DE4 5 F3
Lumshill Rise. DE4 5 E3
Lydford Rd. DE55 14 D2
Lynam Rd. DE56 9 F5
Lyncroft Av. DE5 23 E3
Lynd Clo. NG16 21 H3
Lyndale Dri. DE5 23 G4
Lynholmes Rise. DE4 5 E4
Lynholmes Road. DE4 5 E4
Lynton Clo. DE5 22 C1
Lynton Rd. DE56 9 D8

Magnolia Way. DE55 18 C2
Maid Marian Av. NG16 21 H3
Main Rd, Crich Carr. DE4 8 A3
Main Rd, Jacksdale. NG16 24 B1
Main Rd, Lower Hartshay. DE5 22 A1
Main Rd, Pye Bridge. NG16 20 A3
Main Rd, Underwood. NG16 25 E2
Main Rd, Westwood. NG16 20 D6
Main St, New Brinsley. NG16 25 E4
Main St, Newton. DE55 13 D5
Main St, Sth Normanton. DE55 16 B1
Main St, Wirksworth. DE4 28 A1
Mainside Cres. NG16 25 G3
Makeney Rd, Holbrook Moor. DE56 11 E8
Makeney Rd, Milford. DE56 11 C8
Malpas Rd. DE4 4 C3
Malthouse Clo. DE4 28 B1
Malvern Gdns. DE4 4 D3
Manifold Dri. NG16 21 G3
Manitoba Way. NG16 21 F3
Manor Clo. DE55 13 D5
Manor Ct. DE55 19 G4
Manor Croft. DE5 22 C1
Manor Rd. DE56 10 B4
Mansfield Rd, Alfreton. DE55 14 D4
Mansfield Rd, Lane End. DE55 12 E2
Mansfield Rd, Heanor. DE75 27 F4
Mansfield Rd, Selston. NG16 21 F4
Mansfield Rd, Sth Normanton. DE55 16 B3
Mansfield Rd, Underwood. NG16 25 G3
Manvers St. DE5 22 D3
Maple Av. DE5 22 C4
Maple Dri. DE55 16 B4
Maple Dri. DE56 11 D5
Maple Gdns. DE75 26 D4
Marina Rd. DE75 26 C5
Market Clo. DE55 16 A2
Market Pl. DE56 10 C4
Market Pl. DE5 23 G4
Market Pl, Cromford. DE4 6 C5
Market Pl, Wirksworth. DE4 28 B4
Market Pl, Riddings. DE55 19 G4
Market Pl, Sth Normanton. DE55 16 A2
Market Pl. DE75 27 F4
Market Pl. NG16 19 H6
Market St. DE55 16 A3
Market St. DE75 27 E4
Marlborough Dri. DE56 10 E3
Marsh La. DE56 10 C3
Marsh La Cres. DE56 10 D3
Marshall St. DE55 14 C4
Marshall St. DE75 27 F3
Marston Clo. DE56 10 E1
Martindale Ct. DE56 10 F2
Masson Rd. DE4 6 C2
Matlock Green. DE4 4 D5
Matlock Rd. DE4 8 A3
Matlock Rd. DE56 10 B1
Matt Orchard. DE55 16 C4
Mawkin La. NG16 17 G3
Mayfield Av. DE75 27 E4
Meadow Av. DE5 23 G4
Meadow Bank. DE55 16 A1
Meadow Clo. DE55 12 E1
Meadow Ct. DE56 10 B4
Meadow Ct. DE55 16 A4
Meadow Gro. DE55 13 D5
Meadow La, Alfreton. DE55 14 D3
Meadow La, Sth Normanton. DE55 15 G1
Meadow Rd. DE5 22 D3
Meadow St. NG16 19 H5
Megdale. DE4 4 B3
Melbourne Clo. DE56 11 C5
Melbourne St. NG16 21 H4
*Melton Ct, Cantley Rd. DE55 19 F4
Memorial Croft. DE4 28 C2
Mentmore Clo. DE55 18 C3
Mercer Cres. DE55 15 E5
Merlin Clo. DE56 10 E2
Metro Av. DE55 13 D5
Mettesford. DE4 5 E4
Mews Ct. DE4 5 H4
Mias Clo. DE4 5 H4
Middlebrook Rd. NG16 21 H6
Middleton Rd. DE4 28 A1
Midland Rd. DE75 27 E3
Mill Clo. DE55 18 B3
Mill Holme. DE55 16 C4
Mill La, Holloway. DE4 7 H3
Mill La, Lea Bridge. DE4 7 G6
Mill La. DE5 23 F4
Mill La. DE55 19 E4
Mill La. DE56 10 D4
Mill La. NG16 16 D6
Mill Rd. DE4 6 C5
Mill Rd. DE75 27 G5
Mill St. DE56 10 B3
Mill Yard. DE55 19 E2
Millbank. DE75 27 G5
Milldale Clo. DE5 22 D6
Millers Green. DE4 28 A6
Millersdale Clo. DE56 10 D3
Milner Av. DE5 23 G4
Milton Av. DE55 15 E4
Milward Rd. DE75 26 D3
Minster Way. DE55 18 B3
Mitchell Av. NG16 27 G2
Monk Rd. DE55 15 E5
Monsal Cres. DE55 12 C3
Monsal Dri. DE55 15 H3
Montpelier Rd. DE56 9 D8
Monument La. NG16 24 A1
Monyash Way. DE56 10 D2
Moor Rise. DE56 11 E7
Moor Road. NG16 25 E5
Mooredge Dri. DE4 5 F3
Mooredge Rd. DE4 8 D1
Moorfield. DE4 4 D2
Moorfield Rd. DE56 11 E8
Moorpool Cres. DE56 11 E8
Moorside Clo. DE4 6 B6
Moorside La. DE56 11 E7
Morleyfields Clo. DE5 23 E3
Mornington Rise. DE4 5 E5
Morrel Wood Dri. DE56 10 F2
Moseley St. DE5 22 C2
Moss La. DE5 22 D1
Moulton Clo. DE55 18 C2
Moulton Clo. DE56 10 F3
Mount Cres. DE55 16 A4
Mount Pleasant. DE5 22 C2
Mount Pleasant. DE55 19 F5
Mount Pleasant Dri. DE56 10 A2
Mount St. DE75 27 E4
Mountford Av. DE4 28 B5
Mulberry Mews. DE5 22 C6
Mundy St. DE75 27 E4
Mundys Dri. DE75 27 F5

Nailers Way. DE56 10 E2
Nan Gells Hill. DE4 28 C2
Naseby Rd. DE56 10 F3
Needham St. DE5 23 G4
Nelson St. DE75 27 E3
Nether Clo. DE55 18 B3
Nether Gdns. DE4 28 B4
New Bath Rd. DE4 6 C2
New Breck Rd. DE56 10 C4
New La. DE55 13 F6
New Rd, Belper. DE56 10 B4
New Rd, Bullbridge. DE56 9 E7
New Rd, Codnor. NG16 23 H2
New Rd, Crich. DE4 8 D4
New Rd, Far Laund. DE56 10 E1
New Rd, Ironville. NG16 24 A1
New Rd, Wirksworth. DE4 28 C2
New Row. NG16 20 A5
New St, Alfreton. DE55 14 C4
New St, Hilcote. DE55 13 F8
New St, Matlock. DE4 4 D4

New St, Newton. DE55	13 D5	Orchard La. DE4	4 A1
New St,		Orchard Rd. DE4	6 B2
Somercotes. DE55	19 F2	Orchard Rd. DE55	19 F4
New St, Sth		Ormonde St. NG16	27 H1
Normanton. DE55	16 A1	Ormonde Ter. NG16	27 H1
New St,		Outram St. DE5	22 D2
Swanwick. DE55	18 A3	Over La. DE56	10 F4
New Westwood. NG16	20 D6	Overdale. DE4	5 F4
Newbridge Rd. DE56	9 C8	*Overstone Clo,	
Newham Ct. DE75	27 G4	Naseby Rd. DE56	10 F3
Newlands Cres. DE55	13 D5	Owers Av	27 F6
Newlands Dri. DE55	19 F5	Oxford St. DE5	22 D3
Newlands Dri. DE75	27 F2	Oxford St. DE55	13 B7
Newlands Rd. DE55	19 F5		
Newlyn Dri. DE55	16 C2		
Newnham Av. DE5	22 B3	Paddock Clo. NG16	16 D3
Newstead Clo. NG16	21 H3	Paddocks Clo.. NG16	16 D3
Newton Clo. DE56	10 E2	Padley Clo. DE5	22 C1
Newton Rd. DE5	12 C4	Palmer Dri. DE55	18 A3
Newtonwood La. DE55	12 E4	Palmerston St,	
Nightingale Clo. DE4	7 G5	Jacksdale. NG16	24 D1
Nightingale Clo. DE5	22 C3	Palmerston St,	
Nightingale Cres. NG16	21 H4	Underwood. NG16	25 G2
Nixs Hill. DE55	14 D5	Park Av. DE5	23 E3
Nook End Rd. DE75	27 E4	Park Clo. NG16	16 D6
Norbreck La. DE4	28 A4	Park Dri. DE55	18 B4
Norbury Way. DE56	10 E2	Park La. DE4	8 F2
Norman Rd. DE5	22 B2	Park La, Pinxton. NG16	16 C5
Norman Rd. DE55	19 G3	Park La, Selston. NG16	21 G2
Normanton Av. DE55	15 E5	Park Rd. DE5	22 D3
Normanton Brook		Park Rdl. DE56	11 D5
Rd. DE55	16 D1	Park Side. DE55	19 F3
North Clo. DE56	16 A2	Park St. DE55	22 D3
North End. DE4	28 B4	Park St. DE5	14 C5
North La. DE56	11 A7	Park St. DE75	26 D3
North Par. DE4	6 B2	Park View. DE55	19 F5
North St,		Park Vw. DE75	26 D4
Alfreton. DE55	14 D5	Parkhouse Dri. DE55	15 G3
North St,		Parkin St. DE55	15 E3
Cromford. DE4	6 C5	Parkside. DE56	10 C4
North St,		Parkside Clo. NG16	19 H6
Langley Mill. NG16	27 H2	Parkside Dri. NG16	19 H6
North St,		Pasteur Av. DE5	22 C2
Newton. DE55	13 C6	Pasture La. DE5	13 F7
North St,		Paxton Clo. DE4	4 B3
Pinxton. NG16	17 E5	Peach Av. NG16	21 G4
North St,		Peach Av. DE55	16 B1
Riddings. DE55	19 F4	Peach St. DE75	27 E5
North St, Sth		Peak Av. DE55	19 E4
Normanton. DE55	16 A2	Peak View. DE55	15 H3
Northam Dri. DE5	22 C2	Peakdale Clo. DE5	22 D6
Northern Rd. DE75	26 D3	Pear Tree Av. DE5	22 C4
Nottingham La. DE5	19 G4	Pease Clo. DE55	14 D5
Nottingham Rd,		Pease Hill. DE55	14 D5
Alfreton. DE55	14 D4	Peasehill Rd. DE5	22 D4
Nottingham Rd,		Peatburn Av. DE75	26 D4
Bagthorpe. NG16	25 H1	Peel St. NG16	27 H3
Nottingham Rd,		Peel St. DE55	16 B2
Belper. DE56	10 C4	Pendean Clo. DE55	13 B7
Nottingham Rd,		Pendine Clo. DE55	16 D2
Codnor. DE5	23 H5	Penn St. DE56	10 C3
Nottingham Rd,		Pennine Dri. DE55	15 H3
Ripley. DE5	22 D2	Pennine Av. DE55	19 E3
Nottingham Rd,		Pennine Clo,	
Selston. DE55		Newton. DE55	13 D5
Nursery Gdns. DE55	16 C3	Pennine Clo,	
Nuttal Clo. DE55	14 C5	Tibshelf. DE55	12 C3
Nuttal St. DE55	14 C5	Pennine Dri. NG16	21 F3
		Pennytown Ct. DE55	19 E1
Oak Av. NG16	27 H1	Penryn Clo. DE55	16 D2
Oak Av. DE5	22 C5	Pentrich Rd. DE55	18 A3
Oak Clo. NG16	16 D5	Pentrich Rd. DE5	22 D2
Oak Dri. DE55	14 D3	Peterway. DE55	19 F2
Oak Rd. DE4	4 D4	Peveril Ct. DE5	22 C3
Oak Tree Gdns. DE4	5 H5	Peveril Clo. DE55	19 E4
Oakdale Rd. DE55	16 B4	Peveril Rd. DE55	12 C3
Oakerthorpe Rd. DE4	28 C1	Pewit La. DE55	12 A3
Oakhurst Clo. DE55	10 A2	Philip Way. DE55	19 F2
Oakland St. DE55	14 D4	Piatts Av. DE75	26 D4
Oaklands Av. DE75	27 G3	Pic Tor La. DE4	4 D5
Oaklands Cres. DE55	19 F5	Pillar Butts. DE4	28 B5
Oaksedge La. DE4	5 G3	Pilsley Clo. DE56	10 E2
Oaktree Rd. DE55	18 C2	Pinchoms Hill Rd. DE56	11 D5
Oaktree Rd. DE55	13 F8	Pine Av. NG16	22 C3
Old Chapel La. NG16	25 G2	Pine Clo. DE5	22 C3
Old Coach Rd. DE4	5 E3	Pinewood Av. DE5	23 G5
Old Coppice Side. DE75	27 E6	Pinewood Rd. DE4	4 D2
Old Hackney La. DE4	4 A1	Pinewood Rd. DE56	10 A2
Old Hartshay Hill. DE5	22 C2	Pingle Cres. DE56	10 B3
Old La. DE4	28 B2	Pingle La. DE56	10 B3
Old Lime Ct. DE4	5 E4	Pinxton Green. NG16	17 F5
Old Storth La. DE55	16 C3	Pinxton La. NG16	17 H4
Olde Englishe Rd. DE4	4 D5	Pinxton La,	
Oliver Clo. NG16	27 H3	Pinxton. NG16	17 F2
Ontario Dri. NG16	21 G3	Pinxton La, Sth	
Open Acre. NG16	19 H6	Pinxton. NG16	16 C3
Orange St. DE5	14 D4	Pit La, Ripley. DE5	22 D3
Orchard Clo. DE5	23 F5	Pit La,	
Orchard Cres. DE55	18 A3	Waingroves. DE5	23 F6

Pit Row. NG16	25 G3	Rock House Est. DE4	6 C5
Pittywood Rd. DE4	28 A5	Rodgers La. DE55	14 C4
Plainspot Rd. NG16	25 E3	Roes La. DE4	8 D2
Platt St. NG16	17 E6	Rope Walk. DE5	22 D4
Plumptre Rd. NG16	27 H1	Roper Av. DE75	27 F5
Plymouth Av. NG16	17 E6	Rose End Av. DE4	6 B5
Pond Rd. DE56	11 E8	Rosewood Clo. DE55	16 C1
Pool Clo. NG16	16 D2	Rosewood Cres. NG16	27 H3
Pope Carr Rd. DE4	4 D4	Rosier Cres. DE55	18 C2
Poplar Av. DE5	22 C4	Rothwell La. DE56	10 D4
Poplar Av. DE55	16 B1	Rowan Av. DE5	22 C4
Poplar Ter. NG16	21 F4	Rowan Dri. NG16	20 D3
Porter La. DE4	28 A1	Rowland St. DE55	14 C3
Porterhouse Rd. DE5	23 E3	Rowthorne Av. DE55	18 C2
Portland Rd. NG16	21 G2	Royal Oak Dri. NG16	21 H3
Pottery Clo. DE56	10 E2	Ruffstone Av. DE56	11 E8
Poynter Clo. DE75	26 D4	Rugby Av. DE55	15 E5
Pratthall La. DE4	28 C6	Rutland Av. DE4	4 D3
Preston Av. DE55	15 E4	Rutland Av. DE5	23 F5
Primary Clo. DE56	10 C4	Rutland Rd. NG16	20 C6
Primrose Av. NG16	25 G3	Rutland St. DE4	4 D3
Primrose Clo. DE55	16 C1	Ryegrass Clo. DE56	10 F4
Primrose Hill. DE55	13 B7		
Princess Av. DE55	16 B2	Sacheverall Av. NG16	16 D4
Priory Gdns. DE55	18 C2	St Andrews Clo. DE55	18 D3
Priory Rd,		St Andrews Dri. DE55	18 B3
Alfreton. DE55	15 E3	St Giles Walk. DE4	4 D5
Priory Rd,		St Helens Av. NG16	16 D4
Newton. DE55	13 D6	*St Helens Ct,	
Prospect Av. DE55	15 H3	Lindley St. NG16	21 E4
Prospect Dri. DE4	4 C3	St Helens Dri. NG16	20 D3
Prospect Pl. DE55	11 B5	St Helens La. DE4	28 C5
Prospect Rd. DE75	27 G5	St James Clo. DE56	10 F3
Prospect St. DE55	14 D4	St James Dri. NG16	25 E4
Providence Pl. DE55	14 C5	St Johns Clo. NG16	25 E4
Providence St. DE5	22 D4	*St Johns Clo,	
Pump Clo. DE4	4 B3	Victoria St. DE5	23 E2
Purchase Clo. DE75	26 D3	St Johns Rd. DE4	4 C6
Pye Hill Rd. NG16	20 A5	St Johns Rd. DE56	10 C4
Pytchley Clo. DE56	10 F3	St Johns St. DE4	28 B4
		St Joseph St. DE4	4 D4
Quarry Bank. DE4	4 C2	St Laurence Clo. DE75	27 F3
Quarry La. DE4	5 F2	St Marys Gate. DE4	28 B4
Quarry Rd. DE55	19 F3	St Marys Walk. NG16	24 C1
Quarry Rd. DE56	11 B6	St Michaels Clo. DE55	16 B1
Queen St, Belper. DE56	10 C4	St Thomas Clo. DE55	12 B4
Queen St,		Salcey Clo. DE55	18 B3
Ironville. NG16	19 H6	Salcombe Rd. DE55	15 E3
Queen St,		Saiters La. DE4	4 A5
Pinxton. NG16	16 D5	Samuel Ct. DE4	22 D4
Queen St,		Sandbed La. DE56	11 E5
Somercotes. DE55	19 F2	Sandham La. DE55	22 B4
Queen St, Sth		Sandhill Rd. NG16	25 H2
Normanton. DE55	16 A3	Sandwood Clo. DE55	13 D5
Queen St,		Sandy La, Crich. DE4	8 C4
Waingroves. DE5	23 F5	Sandy La, Matlock. DE4	5 E4
Queens Dri. DE55	26 D3	Sarah Clo. DE55	19 F3
Queens Dri. DE56	10 A2	Saw Pit La. DE55	12 E3
Queens Dri. NG16	25 E5	Saxton Av. DE75	27 F3
Queensview Dri. DE5	23 F5	Scarthin. DE4	6 C5
		School Croft. DE55	19 G4
Raglan St. DE55	14 D4	School La. DE5	22 C3
Ralph Dri. DE55	19 F3	School La. DE55	16 B4
Raven Av. DE55	12 C3	School Rd. DE4	5 E4
*Raven Clo,		School Rd,	
Cantley Rd. DE55	19 F4	Bagthorpe. NG16	25 H1
Raven Oak Clo. DE56	11 E6	School Rd,	
Ravenstor Rd. DE4	28 B2	Selston. NG16	21 G3
Rawson St. NG16	21 G4	Scott Dri. DE55	19 G2
Ray Av. DE75	27 E4	Sedgewick St. NG16	27 H3
Ray St. DE75	27 E4	Sedgwick St. NG16	24 C1
Recreation Clo. DE55	13 B7	Selston Rd. NG16	20 B6
Recreation Rd. DE4	28 A5	Severn Sq. DE55	14 C4
Recreation St. NG16	21 H4	Shakespeare Dri. DE55	15 E4
Red Barn Clo. DE55	13 E5	Sharrard Clo. NG16	25 G3
Red Barn La. DE55	13 E5	Shaw Ct. DE55	19 F4
Red La. NG16	25 E4	Shaw La. DE56	11 B7
Red La. DE55	15 H4	Shawcroft Av. DE55	19 F5
Red Lion Sq. DE75	27 E4	Shaws Hill. DE4	8 B3
Redfern Av. DE5	22 D2	Sheldon Rd. DE75	26 C1
Redgate St. NG16	16 D5	Sheriff Dri. DE4	4 C3
Redmoor Clo. DE5	23 G4	Sheriff La. DE4	4 B3
Regent Ct. NG16	19 H6	Sherwood Rd. DE4	5 E5
Regent St. NG16	27 H3	Sherwood St,	
Reynolds Av. DE55	23 E3	Littlemoor. DE55	13 E5
Riber Av. DE55	5 E3	Sherwood St,	
Riber Clo. DE4	5 H4	Somercotes. DE55	19 E2
Riber Rd. DE4	6 D1	Sherwood Way. NG16	21 H4
Riber View. DE4	5 H4	Shetland Rd. DE55	12 C4
*Richardsons La,		Shireoaks. DE56	10 A2
Newlands Dri. DE55	19 F5	Shirley Dri. DE5	22 C3
Riddings Hill. NG16	19 H6	Shirley Rd. DE55	18 C3
Ridgdale View. DE55	22 C2	Short St. DE56	10 E3
Ridgeway. NG16	27 G6	Shropshire Av. NG16	20 C6
Ridgeway La. DE56	9 E7	*Silken Holme,	
Ridgewood Dri. DE4	6 D5	The Brockwell. DE55	16 B4
Ripley Rd. DE5	22 A3	Sinclair Clo. DE75	26 D5
Ripley Rd. DE56	9 D7	Sitwell Grange	
Roberts Dri. DE55	14 D4	La. DE55	12 A1

Skye Gdns. DE55	12
Slack La. DE5	22
Slack La. DE55	19
Slack La. DE56	9
Slack La. DE75	27
Slade Clo. DE55	16
Slater Cres. DE4	28
Sleetmoor La. DE55	18
Sleights La. DE55	16
Slough La. DE4	28
Slough Rd. DE55	16
Smalley Clo. NG16	25
Smeath Rd. NG16	25
Smedley Av. DE55	19
Smedley St. DE4	4
Smedley St East. DE4	4
Smedley St West. DE4	4
Smeeton St. DE75	27
Smith Av. DE5	28
Smith Dri. NG16	27
Smith Rd. DE4	4
Smuse La. DE4	5
Snitterton Rd. DE4	4
Snowdrop Valley. DE4	4
Snowfield View. DE4	28
Somercotes Hill. DE55	19
Sough La,	
Bolehill. DE4	28
Sough La,	
Wirksworth. DE4	28
South Croft. DE55	14
South End. DE4	6
South Par. DE4	6
South St,	
Newton. DE55	13
South St,	
Riddings. DE55	19
South St, Sth	
Normanton. DE55	16
South St,	
Swanwick. DE55	18
South View,	
Tansley Knoll. DE4	5
South View,	
Wirksworth. DE4	28
Southfields Av. NG16	16
Southfields Dri. DE55	16
Spa Croft. DE55	16
Spencer Av. DE56	10
Spencer Dri. DE55	19
Spencer Rd. DE56	10
Sperry Clo. NG16	16
Spinners Way. DE56	10
Sporton Clo. DE55	16
Sporton La. DE55	16
Spout La. DE4	5
Spring Clo. DE56	10
Spring La. DE75	27
Spring Rd. DE55	19
Springfield Clo. DE4	8
Springfield Cres. DE55	19
Springfield Rise. DE4	5
Springfield Ter. DE5	22
Springfield View. DE5	22
Springhill Way. DE5	23
Spruce Av. NG16	20
Staffa Dri. DE55	12
Stafford Cres. DE4	28
Stainsby Av. DE75	27
Stamford St. DE4	27
Stanley Av. DE5	22
Stanley St. DE55	19
Stanton Av. DE56	10
Stanton Moor Vw. DE4	4
Starkholmes Rd. DE4	4
Starthe Bank. DE75	27
Station La. DE5	23
Station La. NG16	24
Station Rd,	
Langley Mill. NG16	27
Station Rd,	
Pinxton. NG16	17
Station Rd,	
Selston. NG16	21
Station Rd,	
Tibshelf. DE55	12
Steam Mill La. DE5	23
Steep Turnpike. DE4	4
Steeple Grange. DE4	28
Stewart St. DE55	19
Stirland St. DE5	23
Stoddard Dri. DE75	27
Stoke Clo. DE56	10
Stoneleigh Way. DE55	19
Stones La. DE4	8
Stoney Hill. DE4	28
Stoney La,	
Brinsley. NG16	25
Stoney La,	
Selston. NG16	21